JEAN SPRACKLAND

Jean Sprackland's first book of non-fiction, *Strands: A Year of Discoveries on the Beach*, won the 2012 Portico Prize. She is the author of five poetry collections, including *Tilt*, which won the 2007 Costa Poetry Award, and *Green Noise* (2018). She lives in London.

JEAN SPRACKLAND

These Silent Mansions

VINTAGE

1 3 5 7 9 10 8 6 4 2

Vintage is part of the Penguin Random House group of companies whose addresses can be found at global.penguinrandomhouse.com

Copyright © Jean Sprackland 2020

Jean Sprackland has asserted her right to be identified as the author of this Work in accordance with the Copyright, Designs and Patents Act 1988

First published in Vintage in 2021
First published in hardback by Jonathan Cape in 2020

penguin.co.uk/vintage

A CIP catalogue record for this book is available from the British Library

ISBN 9780099587149

Printed and bound in Great Britain by Clays Ltd, Elcograf S.p.A.

The authorised representative in the EEA is Penguin Random House Ireland, Morrison Chambers, 32 Nassau Street, Dublin DO2 YH68.

Penguin Random House is committed to a sustainable future for our business, our readers and our planet. This book is made from Forest Stewardship Council® certified paper.

For my brothers

'Human beings housed their dead before they housed themselves.'
Robert Pogue Harrison, *The Dominion of the Dead*

'The birds in Nunhead Cemetery begin
... There must be some advantage to the light'
Maurice Riordan, 'The January Birds'

'Our story is lost in silence. Go by, mad world!'
Edgar Lee Masters, 'Benjamin Pantier'

Contents

Preface: Old Haunts

I can remember my life by the graveyards I have known. Through the stages of childhood and adolescence, and throughout my adult years, during momentous events and times of tumultuous change, and in the flat calm waters that lay between, there have always been the graveyards. Wherever I have lived, I have found them – some like cities, others like gardens, or forests of stone – and they have become the counterparts of those lived places: the otherworlds which have helped make sense of this world.

When I move somewhere new, going to the graveyard is a way of learning where I am. Later, returning again and again is like listening to a favourite piece of music, hearing it a little differently each time. On holiday, I stroll there as if to the beach or the museum. At the church door after a wedding or a funeral, I look for an excuse to detach myself and wander off among the stones I've glimpsed over the shoulders of my fellow guests or mourners. Churchyard, municipal cemetery, private burial ground: all are places of escape, somewhere to walk and think, and to notice things which are generally overlooked or forgotten. There is always the chance of a random discovery, the opportunity to be surprised by something beautiful or interesting. Sorrow is present, but age and weather have tempered it. A graveyard is softened by ivy and elder, blurred by rain and soot, dismantled gradually by the passing years, always in a state of becoming.

Why are so many of us drawn to these peculiar places, with all their contradictions and intensities of feeling? Quiet, green spaces are precious, of course, and these premises of death are full of life.

Many have evolved into nature reserves, sheltering plants and animals driven to the brink by urban development and intensive agriculture. One of the attractions of the urban graveyard is the chance to observe its ancient trees, the birds and insects that shelter in them, and the lichens that colonise their bark. But it's not only this intrinsic beauty and richness, the tranquillity, the opportunities for solitariness they afford; graveyards are charged with other, compelling kinds of meaning. For many centuries they were crucial, because of the importance of consecrated ground in the mystery of resurrection. They remain, for some people at least, the locations of ritual leave-taking and commemoration. These are liminal places. To enter one is to come into the presence of death, or at least close enough to be confronted with its reality. What makes us want to be there, and what do we hope to find?

Perhaps it begins in childhood. In the village where I grew up, the churchyard served as an unofficial playground. You could be unobserved there, out of sight of the adults. My friend Alison and I used to hide behind gravestones and jump out on younger children, not out of spite or ghoulishness, it seems to me now, but from sheer excess of energy. It was not a scary place to me, and I didn't see why anyone else should find it so either. At seven or eight, I remember sitting cross-legged between the graves with a group of other kids, and learning a song:

> Whenever you see a hearse go by
> Do you think you might be the next to die?
> They wrap you up in a big white sheet
> From the top of your head right down to your feet.
> They wash your face, they comb your locks,
> They strap you down in a big black box.
> They put you in a hole in the ground
> While all your relatives stand around.
> They throw in stones, they throw in rocks,
> They don't give a damn if they break the box.

All goes well for about a week,
But then your coffin begins to leak.
The worms crawl in and the worms crawl out,
They crawl in thin but they crawl out stout.
Your eyes pop out, your teeth decay,
And that's the end of a perfect day.

I would not have sung these words at home. In its own way this was as risqué as everything else the older kids were so keen to teach the younger ones: swearing, smoking, dirty jokes. Of all the songs handed down to us, the ones we sang most boisterously were the morbid ones: 'Found a Peanut', often embellished with extra gruesome details of the effects of the poisoning, the failed operation and the painful death which followed; 'Cocaine Bill and Morphine Sue', with its puzzling final couplet: 'Ashes to ashes, dust to dust. / If the coke don't get you, the morphine must.' I had no idea what morphine was, but I knew coke well enough: the stuff kept in an asbestos bunker by the back door, and shovelled onto the fire to eke out the coal. When I watched my father clearing the grate in the mornings, I would hum it under my breath: *ashes to ashes, dust to dust*.

Out of that early familiarity with my local churchyard grew a lifelong habit of exploring such places. I find quieter pleasures there these days: walking between graves and thinking about the people buried there and the lives they led. I'm less interested in the well-known names – it has always seemed to me that the famous dead can look after themselves – than in the unremarkable and the forgotten, those names which can no longer be deciphered, and those which were never inscribed at all. I think about the span of a human life – how one may be longer than another but all are finite – and how I and everyone around me is part of the inescapable repeating pattern so explicitly demonstrated here. *Born ... Departed this life*. Touching the stones and reading the chiselled names of the dead keeps me acquainted with reality.

But thoughts of my own obliteration are not what preoccupy me as I walk between the stones. Within the eternally repeating pattern, the graveyard reveals endless variations. The mysteries of an ordinary life. Unusual longevity, or a high rate of infant mortality. The rise and fall of a powerful family or a local industry; an epidemic or natural disaster. A burial place is the repository not only of individual stories but also of a collective history: of how human beings have attempted to make sense of death, though it is beyond our comprehension; of our attempts to maintain a relationship with the dead; and of the various services we have hoped they will perform or provide for us. An old graveyard is not inviolable, and does not always endure, but where it does, it seems to speak of continuity in a restless world. Its air of timelessness is not entirely illusory; change has been slower and gentler there. Death and life, past and present are woven together. It works on a different clock. Or perhaps it is itself a kind of clock, locating us in time, showing how the slow years tick by and become centuries, and how each of us fits into the long sequence of generations.

The gravestone, if it still stands, and if weather has not eroded the lettering completely, is often the most solid thing left of a life no less real and meaningful than my own. There may be very little to go on – a name, a date, perhaps a brief message or biblical text, often so familiar it hardly registers – but it can be enough to open up a story about something that happened there: a story which has been forgotten, or suppressed, or was never really told in the first place. Even where there is no stone, there may be a trace – a local legend, a footnote, a rumour – that keeps that story just this side of oblivion. In each of the graveyards I have known best, there's been a name which has infatuated me, a few fragments of story waiting to be pieced together. The name, and the person who answered to it, has stayed with me and accompanied me through my life. It can be hard to tell which of us is haunting the other.

These threads of meaning – awareness of mortality, orientation in place and time, the substance of other lives – came together for me a few years ago, when I moved from the coast to the city and began to explore my new surroundings on foot. When I lived by the sea, I walked either north or south, my route defined by the sound of the waves on my left or on my right. Those empty expanses of sand, where I met only gulls and oystercatchers, could be lonely and disorientating, but with the sea to guide me I was never really lost. In London, I went on walking. But there was no shore to follow, and the city felt edgeless and seething. This time I walked to re-set my internal compass. I went with no particular direction in mind, noticing things with the intensity of the tourist: curiosities, contradictions, tokens and vestiges linking here with elsewhere, then with now.

On one of these expeditions, I arrived at a gate, and behind it a dilapidated churchyard. It was a raw November afternoon, and the path was slippery with black leaves. I picked my way over the broken ground to a marble tomb, and read its loquacious inscription:

STRANGER, WHOE'ER THOU ART THAT VISITETH
THESE SILENT MANSIONS OF THE DEAD, HERE PAUSE –
CONTEMPLATE WITH VENERATION THE ASHES OF A MAN
WHO WAS EVER GENEROUS, KIND AND GOOD –
THE FAVOURITE OF NATURE AND FORTUNE NOW MOULDERS INTO DUST.
HAPPY THOU IF THUS EARLY TAUGHT
THE FRAILTY OF ALL EARTHLY BLISS THOU SEEKEST.

On the grass, a discarded Golden Virginia packet offered its own terse coda: *Smoking Kills.*

I stood shivering near the railings which separate the churchyard from the park, hearing the shouts of children on the adventure playground. At that moment, more acutely aware than usual of the past bubbling up through the cracks in the present, I had the idea of going back.

I am past the middle of my life, I heard myself say. The mansions of the dead kept their silence. It was one of those moments where you see your life as something actual and finite: a long walk, perhaps, and you the walker with more than half the distance covered. A parent has recently died. Your children are living as you once did, as if there were no tomorrow. And then there's you, somewhere in between, wondering how you got here, and trying to reconcile all the irreconcilable bits of your own history, to make a narrative out of those scattered episodes, wanting to look back and see where you've been.

I thought of all the places I had considered home. I haven't had an especially itinerant life; there are not very many of these places, and they are far from exotic. Nevertheless, I felt a kind of thirst for them. Though they were ordinary towns in England, none of them more than a few hours' train journey away, they had acquired in my imagination a patina of strangeness; when I thought of their streets and cafés and parks the colours seemed somehow more saturated than those around me here.

That November afternoon, I decided I must revisit all my old hometowns, to make a journey into the physical fabric of my own past. I couldn't tell whether I would be able to renew my intimacy with them, or whether the turmoil I felt at that prospect was excitement or fear. My own relationship with these places had intensified, grown larger than life and thickened into myth. The shorter my association with a place, and the longer ago, the more it had that unreal and thickened quality. I had remembered and remembered, and like the stone slab over the body of a saint, the place was worn smooth and glassy by the years of pilgrimage.

What I would do now was go back and meet them on their own terms. I wanted to approach these places with humility, and to find out more about some of the other lives lived there. I would return to those remembered names, and search for traces of them in the built environment, in local knowledge and in the written record. I would learn about the river of human experience that rolled under the bridges and between the mills and wharves, in which I was a drop of water, nothing more.

I knew these places would have changed, and I didn't want to go back as if returning from exile, comparing the old with the new and steeping myself in nostalgia. I wasn't interested in that at all. What mattered to me was what the place itself remembered of its past, and what it had forgotten. What remains, and what has been erased.

So I would go in search of my old haunts, I thought. And when I arrived in a city and walked out of the railway station into its altered and indifferent streets, where would I begin?

The graveyard, of course. The realm of meaning, the other-world. Sanctuary of the slow-worm, the fox and the yew. The place where the stories are kept.

I

The graveyard in spring. Pigeons on the lych-gate, spreading their wings in the sun. A woman wheels her bicycle underneath, with a box of red geraniums balanced on the handlebars. The pigeons rise as one and deliver a storm of applause.

Taxus baccata

I am standing under the shaggy roof of a yew tree that is one of the oldest living things in London.

There are several more youthful specimens in this churchyard. One with a trunk smooth as a stockinged leg, another with voluminous skirts which fan out onto the grass, grown through with brambles, studded with ripening fruit. But this one is the matriarch, somewhere around 2,000 years old.

Dating an old yew is not an exact science, especially if the centre has been hollowed out by time. This tree has for hundreds of years been growing up from the ground inside its own shell, nearly twenty-six feet in girth, a measurement which has not changed for at least three centuries.

The bole is a sheath of dead wood, extravagantly whorled and latticed, burred and blistered. In places it's worn quite thin, and the holes are ragged and elongated, as if in the distant past the wood had been through some other more elastic state, and someone had pushed their fingers into its fabric and stretched it until it tore. Elsewhere it thickens like rock, leaning slabs riven with deep parallel cracks.

There are arches and windows with a view of the open heart. One craggy rift is like the mouth of a cave, curtained with hoary old cobweb.

Inside, this single tree is its own small wood. There's a floor of humus and dead needles, and out of it rise many vertical branches, criss-crossed with lateral growth. I think of the 'intertwisted fibres serpentine / Up-coiling, and inveterately convolved', observed by

Wordsworth on the ancient yew at Lorton Vale. Some of these branches are wound like massive coils of rope heaped on a quay.

There would be room for several children to play and hide in this hollow space, and in the eighteenth century a foundling was abandoned here. But this tree's most enduring relationship is with the dead. Some of its lowest branches rest proprietorially on a large chest tomb, and other graves huddle close, sheltered – or swallowed – by its perpetual shade. A memento mori has been left at its foot: the jawbone of a sheep, picked white and gleaming by a fox, and dropped on the grass between two deeply sunken headstones.

Claims and counter-claims are made, but no one knows for sure why yew trees are so common in churchyards. The association of the yew with death and mourning goes back before written language, and its beginnings are lost to us. In more recent centuries there was a belief that it had the capacity to absorb or neutralise noxious vapours emanating from buried corpses.

Writing about the ancient yew in his own village of Selborne, Gilbert White said that 'it seems to have seen several centuries, and is probably coeval with the church, and therefore may be deemed an antiquity'. But his yew was much older than he thought; when it was felled by a gale and its roots dug out, thirty human skeletons were unearthed, some of them 800 years old. That tree, like this one, was there before the church. It must have been an important species in pre-Christian times, in ways we can only really speculate about, and as Christianity spread and churches were built, the planting of yews provided some kind of continuity from the pagan religion it had replaced. Some of its earlier significance was adopted, assimilated or dismantled in the process.

It's easy to imagine why it might have been considered so powerful. It's evergreen, and like holly and mistletoe it acts as a reminder that life endures, even in the depths of winter. An individual tree can live so long as to seem immortal.

And it is of course deadly poisonous, a property which must have been understood from the earliest times. When an agent of death was needed, the yew was a readily available source: for suicide, and for tipping the arrows before hunting or warfare. This was both a tree of death, and a tree of long life.

Every part of the yew is rich in the powerful poison taxine, with the exception of the flesh of the red fruit, which may be eaten if the seed is carefully removed. The wood, the bark and the needles are still occasionally consumed with lethal results – sometimes accidentally, but more often deliberately. Fifty grams of yew needles is considered a fatal dose, and some people have died from much smaller amounts. The wood burns with a fierce heat, and is highly prized for turning and carving, though both sawdust and smoke can induce nausea and palpitations. As Gilbert White observed, the male yew 'in the spring sheds clouds of dust, and fills the atmosphere around with its farina', and even this pollen can cause symptoms. Pliny claims in his *Natural History* that people have been known to die after drinking wine stored in vessels made from yew wood, and that even to sleep under a yew tree is to risk death.

Wordsworth tells us that the Lorton yew was 'of vast circumference and gloom profound', and this species is frequently thought of as forbidding or depressing. I suppose they are not the most elegant of trees – they tend to be stout and heavy, and when they are in their prime the foliage is dense, the growth of needles thick and close. The breeze cannot provoke them into dancing and fluttering; there is no spangling of leaves in the light.

Instead, a yew holds its shape, nurturing shadow and stillness. It has a solid kind of presence, more contemplative than vivacious, not continually rackety with birds but nevertheless a tolerant host to thrushes and finches, who eat the fruit and pass the poisonous seeds undigested.

I like its quiet character, its dark inner space, its coolness on a hot day. And it is not without delicacy. The bark of this venerable specimen is a richly textured palette of browns and purples, streaked with pink and green. Its needles are dark and glossy, vibrant where the growth is new. Some of its lower branches are softened by grey-green lichen. Higher up, spiders have slung their silk trapezes, which tremble and glisten in the sun.

The light glances on something metal, and when I look closer I see a nail driven into the wood. I'm familiar with the myth that hammering nails into an unwanted tree will kill it, but why would anyone want to get rid of this grand old individual?

Later, when I look again at Pliny, I read this: 'I find it recorded that a yew tree is rendered harmless if a copper nail is hammered into the tree.' Is it possible that at some moment in the tree's past, for desperate reasons now lost to memory, someone went to the churchyard with hammer and nail and tried to neutralise its power?

By Flaming Tortures Tried

'Stoke Newington is the perfect place in which to stay lost.'

Iain Sinclair, *Lights Out for the Territory*

Someone has been picking daffodils in Clissold Park, bringing them into St Mary's churchyard next door and placing them on the flat tombs, weighing down the stems with chunks of brick. They lie bruised and gaudy against the wet surfaces, like splashes of spring sunlight with all its brash hesitancy. Someone has been reclaiming the graves, tearing a space in the brambles, marking out a muddy plot in front of an illegible stone here and there. Burnt-out tea-light, pigeon's feather, budding twigs in a vodka bottle. Who has taken the trouble to tend to the long-forgotten dead?

Away from the fence and the park, through a crooked gate and deep in the jungly interior, the day's fabric thins and the present loosens its grip. The noise of the street recedes into the distance, and the voices of children on the adventure playground are softened and filtered. There are no flowers on the family tomb of William Pickett, alderman and sometime Mayor of London. The box of pale stone is in classical style, simply decorated with ornamental pilasters and mounted on a plinth whose iron railings have been pulled like teeth, leaving a row of small depressions scooped and half-healed by the years. A breeze ripples the roof of the tomb with shadow. The lower branches of a holly tree languish exhaustedly over its surface, like the thin arms of a girl over her books.

William's name was once recorded on this stone ledger, but the surface has lain open to the weather for over two centuries, and long ago became inscrutable. Squinting across it at eye level, I can just make out faint bumps and hollows which are all that's left of the text, punctuated with sycamore pollen and bird shit. I move and try a different angle. I have found that a new turn of light or shade can sometimes coax an inscription into view, like the invisible writing children used to make with lemon juice then warm into life over a candle. But no, this cipher is beyond such magic: William has gone.

An inscription to his daughter has endured, however, on an oval tablet on the south side of the tomb, perhaps made of some other more resistant stone. The lettering is large and elegant, in a Caslon typeface all the rage at the time and still clear enough to be admired. I part the undergrowth, clear a space where I can kneel and read the words:

ELIZABETH PICKETT

Died 11th Dec 1781 Aged 23 Years
in consequence of her Cloaths taking Fire
the preceeding Evening.

It's only a snippet of detail, a handful of words. But here in the stillness, under the ragged canopy of holly, it seems eloquent enough to suspend time, just for an instant. The lapsed and forgetful centuries are held like a breath, and a door swings open in my imagination. A lamp-lit room, a winter evening, a fire hissing and popping in the grate. A young woman – not much different in age from my own daughter – standing close for warmth, talking, or reading a letter, or laughing, or just quietly thinking her own thoughts.

A police siren dopplers past, and the door slams shut. I came here to examine this old tomb, and the task is not yet complete. I start pulling away at the roots and rubbish, brushing the soot from the stone with my gloved hand. There's a second inscription about Elizabeth somewhere, a more practical message from the past, a kind of public safety announcement. It's supposed to be underneath the first, but there's nothing there. Where can it be? I pause for a moment, wondering whether I might have misunderstood. I wrote it down somewhere. I peel off my gloves, unzip my rucksack and retrieve my notebook. I copied it out from a blog about London walks, where I first happened across it a week or two back. Yes, here it is, jotted with a temperamental biro – I see where I had to stop and lick the nib and scribble hard to get it going again:

> Reader, if you should ever witness such an afflicting scene,
> recollect that the only method to extinguish the flame,
> is to stifle it with an immediate covering.

When I first read those words and jotted them down so hurriedly, something flashed into view in my mind, something from my deep past. It took me a moment to work out what it was: a book of some kind, a vestige of childhood. I recognised it, to my surprise, as *The Brownie Guide Handbook*, an early 1970s edition. I recalled it as vividly as if I held it in my hands that very morning: the jacket design of yellow and brown, its paper coarsely textured to the touch, and the place inside where I had written my name in Burnt Sienna pencil crayon, along with 'Imps', the name of my Six. Until that moment, I hadn't thought of this volume for forty years or more, but suddenly I remembered that within its pages I had encountered something peculiarly like this monumental inscription of 1781. It was a step-by-step guide, with illustrations. I felt sure some of the words were the same: extinguish, stifle, immediate. I recalled too our old coal fire in its brown-tiled hearth, with the metal fireguard you had to remember to put on when you left the room, and the paraffin heater my grandfather would bring in from the garage and drag screeching across the kitchen lino in winter. I recalled a long night when I lay miserably awake, stiff with fear, having overheard our neighbour Mrs Birkin read out a newspaper story about a poor girl in Derby who stood too close to the fire in her nightdress. I tried to console myself with the knowledge that mine, red brushed nylon with the St Michael logo, had a label sewn into the seam that said FLARE-FREE. I turned on the light and once again studied the drawings in the handbook carefully, in preparation for the day when I would surely be called upon to use my quick wits and roll a blazing victim in a carpet. But the carpet in the picture was nothing like ours, which I had investigated before bedtime and found to be fitted with tacks and gripper rods, and I couldn't see how I would be able to detach it in time. My mouth was dry with foreboding. The instructions were incomplete. For the first time, I confronted the awful thought that *even with the handbook, death might not be averted.*

A handbook is a standard means of dispensing health and safety advice, but chiselling words into stone is rather less orthodox. The advice we expect to read in the churchyard is generally of another kind: exhortations to repent of our sins, to turn away from the vanities of this world and to prepare for the next. I came here keen to see this peculiar inscription for myself, and to photograph it if the light was good enough. But I can't find any sign of it. Since I first encountered it on the blog, I've traced it to several other sources – a history of Middlesex, a compilation of unusual epitaphs. What's more, when I asked a neighbour, Stoke Newington born and bred, she said oh yes, she knew it, it was very unusual and I must go and see. I make another careful circuit, picking my way through the brambles and stones, pulling back the matted vegetation around the base, feverishly examining every surface for clues. On the north side, I can make out a few intriguing words about a son, brother to Elizabeth, slain by pirates in the Bay of Bengal. On either end the words are completely eaten up by rain and soot, and must have been unreadable for many years. There is no address to the reader, no word of advice. On the question of fire safety, the stone has lost its tongue.

I know I'm in the grip of another infatuation. Elizabeth Pickett has got into my head and will not be leaving any time soon. But kneeling again on the damp ground, feeling the cold seep up through the knees of my jeans and into my bones, it occurs to me that the inscription may never have existed at all. Perhaps it was an eighteenth-century urban myth. Perhaps my neighbour read about it, just as I did, and it stuck, and over time she somehow came to believe she'd seen it with her own eyes. Memory is more creative than it feels, the process of remembering an act of construction each time it happens. It's easy to be deceived, to hear or read about something and later to mistake that for first-hand experience. I close the notebook and put it back in my bag. I don't think I'll tell her about this. No one wants to feel they can't rely on their own memory. It's like seeing the surface of a gravestone spalling away, words and all, and glimpsing the blankness underneath.

St Mary's churchyard doesn't attract many visitors; they all make for nearby Abney Park, one of London's Magnificent Seven: an early non-conformist cemetery, now a sprawling and tumbledown place of wingless angels and toppled urns. There are winding paths cut through the undergrowth, and whichever you follow, you arrive before long at the graveside of some eminent scientist, writer or dissident churchman. The founders of the Salvation Army are buried here, and a column in memory of the hymn-writer Isaac Watts thrusts up at the centre like a stone lightning rod. Like so many English graveyards, it is dominated by relics of the Victorian preoccupation with death and burial. The craze for elaborate funerals and ostentatious memorials has left us with a legacy of decaying funerary landscapes and architecture. It's beyond our resources to preserve it all.

Here in the quiet backwater of St Mary's, a makeshift fireplace has been assembled from roof tiles and bits of broken headstone, where all that's left of the sacrifice is a pile of white ash. Condom wrappers lie among the nettles and broken glass, and a rain-soaked sleeping bag slumps against the railings. The windows of the church are wired and barred, but a remnant of copper is exposed where the roofing metal has been peeled back and torn off. This is not a picturesque ruin; it lacks that gothic glamour which attracts the film-makers and poets in their long black coats. It's a more shadowy and secretive place.

St Mary's is the last surviving Elizabethan church in London: a remnant of Stoke Newington's earlier life as a country village, a place of woods and farms and muddy lanes. The building was extended and reconfigured over the centuries in a patchwork of different styles and materials, giving it a makeshift appearance from some angles: delicate stone-tracery windows; grey, rendered tower with mock crenellations; sober Victorian brick. It had to be rescued with a major programme of renovation in the nineteenth century, after a structural survey identified that the roof was rotten and the drains in a state of collapse. Coffins were found to be floating on deep floodwater under the floor, like lost boats drifting on the river Acheron. Soon afterwards, a new church was built across the road, large enough to accommodate the growing congregation, and the old church began its long decline, bombed and vandalised, frequented by rats and damp, until it was saved once more and born again as an arts centre.

Cities need their graveyards. If we lose our urban burial places, we risk creating what Ken Worpole has described in his book *Last Landscapes* as 'cities without memory, cities in denial of death and humanity'. We need their green spaces of refuge, which are not so aggressively tidied and clipped that there's no room for life in them. So much of our common land has been lost to private ownership. In a city there are few public places which are left open day and night, and charge no entry fee, and can be entered freely even when parks and gardens are locked shut.

Open access inevitably means that urban churchyards have a night life. The evidence lies scattered among the official clutter of broken stone and metal crosses and green glass chips, until a band of volunteers come on the second Saturday of the month with their bin bags and protective gloves. And it's not just humans who haunt this place at night. Foxes have dug their way into these silent mansions, letting air into the closed chambers, rearing their young among the ancient dead. I crouch by an unsealed vault and peer down into one of their stone earths, but it's as dark as a mineshaft.

Still, the foxes may be swift and resourceful, but they too succumb in the end: this morning, under a flowering cherry with new blossom the colour of bubble-gum, a vixen lies open-mouthed, the long rows of teeth exposed, the eye sockets empty and blackened.

In the year of Elizabeth Pickett's premature death, the parish of Stoke Newington acquired its first fire engine. It was a wagon mounted with an open trough, with two pistons attached to large handles. Buckets would be brought to fill the trough, and the handles would be pumped up and down, squeezing the pistons and forcing the water out of a leather hose. Until an engine-house was built a few years later, the fire engine was kept here at the church; when the men were called to fight a blaze in one of the surrounding lanes, they would come along this path, right past the Pickett tomb, close enough to brush against the fine new stonework and to catch sight of the inscription by the light of their lanterns as they heaved the wagon, clattering, over the cobbles.

Fifty years later, St Mary's was used by Edgar Allan Poe as the model for the church in his story 'William Wilson'. William looks back on his time as a schoolboy in 'a misty-looking village of England', where he hears 'the deep hollow note of the church-bell, breaking, each hour, with sullen and sudden roar, upon the stillness of the dusky atmosphere in which the fretted Gothic steeple lay imbedded and asleep'. Poe spent three formative years in Stoke Newington, as a pupil at a boarding school down the road, and attended church services here along with his masters and fellow pupils. It's a shame he was too early to know about the coffins adrift on the dark water, right beneath the place where he knelt so often. He'd have made something of that. But at least I can imagine him, on his way back from church one Sunday morning, crossing the open, grassy space of the churchyard, pausing and reading about the fatal fire.

A low rumbling crescendo behind me seems for a moment to herald movement underground: heavy doors rolling apart or subterranean horses approaching at a gallop. But it's just a suitcase being wheeled along the path between the graves, cutting through from the main road to the park and the residential streets beyond. The path is a route of choice for pedestrians and cyclists, though there is an antiquated sign screwed to the railings that reads *Cycling Prohibited By Order*. It's a thoroughfare, rather than a place to wander and explore; a shortcut that offers a scrap of green space, a moment's respite on the way from one appointment to the next. Against the boundary fence, there is a row of huge tombs shrink-wrapped in ivy, like the remnants of an ancient civilisation being swallowed by the encroaching jungle. I suppose it would be possible, with a concerted effort, to bring them back – perhaps even to read their inscriptions – but ivy is so tough and uncompromising, once it has something in its grasp it doesn't let go without a fight. I don't think anyone will bother. However eloquent the messages on those monoliths, they're lost to us now.

Ghastly deaths make popular reading, and all the more so if they involve young women. News of Elizabeth Pickett's death got around. A newspaper report a few days after the event laid out the scene:

Monday night, as Miss Pickett, daughter of Mr Pickett of Ludgate-Hill, was standing by the fire, a spark flew unobserved upon her apron, which almost in an instant set it in a blaze, and communicated to her gown, handkerchief, and cap, with the most astonishing rapidity. Unhappily there was no person in the room but Mr Pickett, who, for a few moments, was bereft of all sense and motion. The fire was extinguished with much difficulty, although several people who were in the house, alarmed at the noise, had come to their assistance. The unfortunate young lady was immediately carried to her bed, where she remained for 12 hours in the most excruciating torture, and then expired.

A few days later, in another paper, the same account was reproduced word for word but with an extra paragraph inserted, elaborating on the horror from the father's point of view: 'In this situation the unfortunate young lady flew to him for relief, and roused at length from a situation no words can describe, he struggled, at the imminent hazard of his life, to stifle the flames, and save his daughter.'

The story was repeated here and there, and before long it had become a sensation. Alternative versions emerged, each painting a different scene, each more touching or more provocative than the last. Elizabeth was depicted in her underwear, dressing or undressing by the fire, when the fatal spark leapt out. Or in an act of filial tenderness, rolling up her father's hair, or bending to cover his face with a handkerchief as he slept. Then the domesticity was turned up a notch or two, and a tantalising extra detail introduced: she was described attending to duties with the box-iron, lifting the red-hot metal 'slug' from the grate when it slipped from the tongs and fell into her stays. She died that day, or the next, or after three days of anguish. She pleaded with her stricken father not to blame himself, or she never spoke another word.

'The scene must have made an indelible impression on the mind of an affectionate parent,' wrote one journalist. This at least has the hallmark of truth. In the aftermath of an accident like this, any parent would wish to salvage something from their daughter's horrible and unnecessary death, to find some meaning in it, to put their own feelings of failure and guilt to some use, to save others from going through the same anguish. As a mother myself, I feel the force of that wish. Isn't that why I'm kneeling here so long, among the rotting leaves and sodden plastic bags, staring at a mute stone surface and willing it to speak?

A tree surgeon is at work in the park, high in a sycamore very close to the railings which separate it from the churchyard. He jokes and banters with his mate below, who keeps a nervous eye on the plastic safety fencing and the families strolling past with buggies and scooters. The chainsaw keens and judders as it runs through a huge branch, easy as slicing bread. I watch the branch fall, and the sight of it breaks last night's dream. I had been decapitated, and I was standing and looking at my own headless body in a mirror, naked and upright and pale as Portland stone. I looked for a long time, completely still and fascinated. I supposed it must be me I was looking at, though I hardly recognised myself. Then, after what felt like hours of staring, it occurred to me to wonder how, without my eyes or my brain, I was able to see my reflection, and logic broke the spell and woke me.

A dream like that could be a sign that I spend too much time in graveyards, I tell myself. Or perhaps it has to do with change, with my recent experience of transplanting myself and recognising who I am and where I fit in this new place. I've been thinking a lot about belonging. I've only lived round here for a few years, so my claim to belonging is a frail one. But more than half the population probably feels the same. This area has seen its fortunes rise in recent years, and property prices have rocketed; nevertheless, the defining demographic is one of movement: arrivals and departures, lettings and changing of locks, livings made or scraped then swapped for somewhere else. Most of the people I see walking down the street, waiting at the bus stops, sitting in the park, going in and out of the shops, are newer here than I am.

There are advantages to newness. Several years on, I can still go out for a walk and chance upon streets and squares and gardens I didn't know were there. I can still make discoveries and be surprised by what I find. I can observe things from the outside, with a degree of detachment. Familiarity has not yet blurred them.

One of the things I notice in this churchyard is how many of the grand monuments are completely bare. Their inscriptions have succumbed to the attentions of time and London weather. At its most complete, the process resembles renovation rather than disfigurement; some tombs have been scrubbed to such uniform smoothness that they look like models in a showroom or, at the grander end of the scale, show-houses on a new estate.

Others still bear their messages, or parts of them. I'm startled by a grey squirrel which leaps down onto a nearby tomb and freezes for a second or two. The immense lid is chained shut with cobwebs. *Family vault*, it says, and nothing more. The rest has been lost. But that short phrase, 'family vault', like 'family home', is resonant with confidence, with a sense of belonging, structure and solidity. The squirrel springs away lightly onto a neighbouring slab, whose principal dedications have been supplemented with others, added later and in much smaller lettering here and there, as if someone were sketching out a rudimentary family tree.

This place is a time machine. Here I am, at the heart of Hackney: hectic, connected, a turmoil of comings and goings. A piece in the jigsaw of North London boroughs, slotted in between Tower Hamlets and Haringey, recently declared 'the most plural and various spot on the planet'. Yet this is unmistakeably a village churchyard, and I stand among the graves of long-established local families – families who had been resident for as long as anyone could trace them back; people who would not have given any thought to questions of belonging, because they knew where their ancestors were and how they themselves fitted into the pattern. *Wife of ... son of ... and also.*

That sense of continuity must have been part of Elizabeth Pickett's experience of this place. But soon after her death, the population began to grow and diversify. The turn of the nineteenth century was a time of social upheaval. The population of London doubled in forty years, and the ripples of change flowed outwards to nearby villages such as Stoke Newington. They too began to attract significant numbers of new arrivals, who were integrated, however slowly and partially, into the local community. Here in the churchyard there is evidence that the 'misty-looking village of England', like its much altered and extended church, was gradually becoming more heterogeneous. A grand tomb close to the church door, for instance, commemorates John Furtado, the son of Portuguese refugees. His father, Isaac, who died in 1801, is also said to be buried here, but if a memorial marks the place it is no longer legible; perhaps it's one of those now consumed by ivy. Isaac was a Sephardic Jew who came to England from Portugal to escape persecution, and worshipped at Bevis Marks synagogue in the City, but after a bitter argument he cut all links there and had his children baptised into the Church of England.

I wonder what such a dramatic break with his religious and cultural inheritance meant to Isaac. Did he experience it as a loss, or was he able to exchange one sense of community for another? What does it mean, anyway, to belong somewhere? During the Industrial Revolution, in that period of mass migration from countryside to town, it was sometimes said that the new immigrants did not belong because they had no dead in the churchyard. The right of belonging in a place could only be earned by dying there. Walking in graveyards, I touch again and again on my own feeling of non-belonging, as if probing a wound in the mouth with the tongue. No place owns me, and I like staying free, staying lost. But I don't know where the bones of my ancestors lie, and I have never seen a monument bearing my family name.

William Pickett's own death was not sudden and dramatic like his daughter's, but pitifully slow and ordinary. It began with a small and insignificant pimple on his back, which grew slowly but unstoppably until it became a carbuncle of enormous size. It baffled a succession of doctors, who could do nothing more than pronounce it incurable.

William's life makes one of those stories of social mobility which seem wildly improbable now. He was born in humble circumstances, the son of a tallow-chandler, and was orphaned by the age of fourteen. Instead of continuing in his father's footsteps, he left the village of Stoke Newington to seek his fortune in London. There he was apprenticed to a goldsmith, discovered he had a talent for business, and set up shop under the sign of the Golden Salmon on Ludgate Hill, manufacturing and selling watches, jewellery, plate, swords and canes. The business grew quickly, and he became a man of means, wealthy enough to build himself a country mansion in Essex, and to commission this grand family tomb, dedicated first to his parents, who had like so many others been buried in unmarked graves. Meanwhile, his political fortunes rose with his material ones: he was elected first an alderman and then Lord Mayor of London.

He had strong opinions about the fabric of the city, its monuments and street layouts. He saw himself as a great moderniser, but he pursued his causes too zealously and put others off. He gained a reputation for stubbornness and eccentricity, and was lampooned in the press: depicted as an outsider, a self-made man, not of the right class. His one success was the demolition of Butcher's Row, a dilapidated street of Elizabethan shops on the Strand, known to coachmen as the Straits of St Clement's because it was too narrow for two vehicles to pass. Here at last was his opportunity to leave a legacy. He threw everything he had into the campaign, and eventually Butcher's Row was razed and replaced by Pickett Street. But by then he was dead. And before long Pickett Street itself was demolished, and his name fell into obscurity.

Only one of William's eight children survived him; the rest were wiped out by a succession of diseases and misadventures. After his own death, the mansion in Essex was put up for sale. The auction listing described it as 'an exceedingly good family house, with all requisite offices, coach-houses, stables, barns, row-houses, and other out-buildings, large kitchen-garden well planted, pleasure-grounds, lawns, plantations, canal, and fish-ponds, and several closes of rich meadow and arable land, containing altogether upwards of forty-six acres'. Over the next 150 years, this desirable estate was bought and sold a dozen times by a succession of well-heeled commuters and their families. Then in 1937 it was acquired by Queen Mary College for a sports centre. A bus took students the twenty-five miles from Mile End in East London twice a week to make use of its playing fields, tennis courts and clubrooms.

Later, large numbers of the dead made that same journey. In the 1970s, at a time when the college was expanding rapidly and urgently needed more space, it sought to negotiate the purchase of a piece of land which would allow it to extend its Mile End campus. There was a snag: three acres of the land in question were occupied by a historic Jewish burial ground, belonging to the Sephardic community at Bevis Marks. There was bitter opposition to the sale, and negotiations were slow and difficult, but eventually a deal was signed. However, the purchase was subject to restriction. The newer extension of the cemetery must not be disturbed, and the college was bound to protect and maintain it in perpetuity. The older section could be cleared, and the graves exhumed and re-sited, freeing the land for construction.

I have seen what's left of the Mile End cemetery, now completely contained and enclosed within the college campus, boxed in like a quadrangle by buildings of mixed vintage and style. The original cemetery wall of London brick still stands along one edge, a mellow old relic among the plate glass and prefabricated panels that surround it. Students pass from one side to the other on a stone-flagged walkway with a parapet of red steel. There are steps down to the stones, which lie horizontal in the gravel, their surfaces deeply eroded by the rain which has pooled on them for a hundred winters or more. Bright green moss has grown in the wet incisions, making them glow like illuminated letters in a medieval manuscript. All the inscriptions are comparatively recent, none earlier than the middle of the nineteenth century, since the site of the older part of the cemetery has disappeared underneath the library and faculty buildings. Before construction began, the remains of 7,000 men, women and children buried between 1733 and 1855 were disinterred, loaded into vehicles and conveyed to their new resting place: the grounds of the sports centre at Dytchleys, William

Pickett's old estate, where they were reburied in mass graves near the edge of his forty-six acres.

I wonder whether William ever met Isaac Furtado, who stormed out of the Bevis Marks synagogue, and whose mortal remains ended up so unexpectedly close to his own in St Mary's churchyard. He certainly knew Bevis Marks, and had acquaintances and business contacts among its congregation. Their paths would have crossed from time to time on Threadneedle Street or Cornhill, as they walked to prayer and he to his mayoral residence at Mansion House. I imagine them passing like ghosts. He lifts his hat and exchanges a greeting as they go by, and neither he nor they can possibly anticipate that one day, long after their deaths, his close of rich meadow will provide a resting place for their bones.

The poet Anna Laetitia Barbauld did not really belong here either. Her family home was Leicestershire, and she only came to live in Stoke Newington towards the end of her life, carried on that turn-of-the-century wave of migration, bringing her dissenting views and unusual life experience with her. Her tomb, which stands close to the railings separating the churchyard from the street, is not a thing of beauty. It's a solid, utilitarian structure of brick, topped with a dark granite slab. Near one end, and off-centre, a mysterious hole, perfectly circular, is cut into the stone.

Similarly off-centre is Barbauld's best-known work, 'The Rights of Women', a tricky and disorientating poem which urges women to make use of their natural femininity to challenge male power. Is it an affirmative response to Mary Wollstonecraft's radical manifesto, or a reaction against it? Readers have long puzzled over its ambiguities, listened carefully for tone of voice and irony:

> Go forth arrayed in panoply divine,
> That angel pureness which admits no stain;
> Go, bid proud Man his boasted rule resign,
> And kiss the golden sceptre of thy reign.

Thinking of that poem now, I'm unexpectedly reminded of the epitaph to his daughter that William Pickett had inscribed on the family tomb, though time has obliterated it. The sentiment may be different, but it's couched in remarkably similar language:

SO UNAFFECTED, SO COMPOS'D A MIND,
SO FIRM, YET SOFT, SO STRONG, YET SO REFIN'D,
HEAVEN, AS PURE GOLD, BY FLAMING TORTURES TRIED:
THE ANGEL BORE THEM, BUT THE MORTAL DIED.

The claim to perfection and the vocabulary of gold and angels bring these two pieces of verse into a kind of alignment, though they are quite different in purpose. The effect of all that impossibly clean and shiny imagery is to lengthen the distance still further and to make the subject inaccessible. Of course we learn nothing about Elizabeth herself. There is nothing to learn. She has vanished, along with her world of stays and box-irons, leaving only a few marks commissioned by her father to be chiselled into stone. Meanwhile, so much has been effaced: the Mile End cemetery emptied and built over; the old church bombed and rebuilt; the tombs swallowed up by ivy; the public-safety inscription either eradicated or non-existent to begin with. Glancing back at the wilted daffodils and other offerings on the old graves near the park railings, I recognise them for what they are: small, random acts of defiance against erasure.

Her father's life has left a faint trace, though not the legacy he so badly wanted. Elizabeth's is stripped to a few bare facts: birth date, death date, a scrap of grisly information about the circumstances. What else is there to know? She was the daughter of an alderman. She was that young woman who went up in flames. All that survives of her is her death, and the way it touches people like me, passing through the churchyard on our way somewhere, catching sight of the inscription and stopping to read, and wondering about her. I stand for a minute, steadying myself against the tomb. I survey the churchyard with my eyes narrowed, deliberately blurring the focus, trying to reset the picture and catch sight of her here: an actual person, embodied and real. The best I can conjure up is a rather translucent figure in sprigged muslin (though 1780 may be too early for sprigged muslin), her arm through the arm of someone (father, brother), walking over the grass between the gravestones. The stones are much sparser than today, of course, and all bright and legible. Not one of them is more than fifty years old; all the names are still known to the living, none has yet slipped beyond memory. The church is already ancient, and much smaller than it is now, and its spire is still made of wood. But the village is growing fast; it will soon fill up the churchyard. Not so long ago, says her father, all this was open fields … and that's as far as I can get before the screen goes wavy and the figures dissolve, like a change of scene in a bad costume drama.

Stone, so solid and lasting, seems to offer the best chance of saving something important and true so that it stays remembered. If the fire safety message ever existed, it could have done some good in the world, stood as a kind of legacy. Perhaps it did anyway, since real or not it was quoted all over the place. It must have stuck in the minds of some of its readers, just as the page in *The Brownie Guide Handbook* glued itself into mine.

Either way, William did what little he could against oblivion. But a story like that spreads as readily as fire itself, and the facts get muddled surprisingly quickly. It's not just that there are many versions of what happened that day; or that Elizabeth is a fugitive figure. It's that sometimes she is excised altogether. Around the turn of the twentieth century, the story began to do the rounds once more in magazines and gazetteers, complete with the epitaph. But with the passage of time the angelic qualities of refinement and composure slipped their moorings somehow, and the trial by flames was no longer hers to bear. The verse was identical, but now it was published under a different heading: 'An epitaph for Mr Wm Pickett – burnt to death'.

Memento Mori

'Corpses show me what I permanently thrust aside in order to live.'

Julia Kristeva, *Powers of Horror*

This old stone resembles an old-fashioned headboard, with a carved skull on each end like a pair of bed-knobs. They have been softened and sculpted by weather and time until they could almost be made of melted candlewax, eye sockets scooped smooth, grin healed over.

I could rest a hand quite comfortably on each of those sleek grey pates, but for the unambiguous message they bring me, down the long centuries. They are testimony to the inexorable facts of death; a reminder, should I need one, that my flesh will rot.

This stone was rubbed clean of its words long ago. But the image of the skull is often found decorating this stern address:

> Remember, stranger passing by:
> As you are now, so once was I;
> As I am now, so shall you be;
> Therefore prepare to follow me.

The classic riposte, on a day when you're feeling strong and life seems to stretch endlessly ahead, goes like this:

> To follow you I'd be content,
> If only I knew which way you went.

But on another day, in a different mood, to pause and read those familiar words accompanied in traditional style with a skull and a pair of crossed bones, is to feel an icy hand brush the back of your neck, though you know very well you are alone.

The skull serves too as a label, illustrating the grave's contents, a visual note of what is and is not included. *Here lieth not the person you knew and loved, but their bones*. I could take some comfort from that, as others seem to take from that sentimental poem so fashionable at funerals a few years ago: 'Do not stand at my grave and weep. / I am not there. I do not sleep ...'

The received wisdom is that nothing shocks us these days; we like to think of ourselves as less constrained by taboo, less inhibited, less flinching in the face of explicit images. But where death is concerned, the skull motif suggests otherwise. It suggests that our eighteenth-century forebears confronted the physical reality more readily than we do. Ever since then, the gaze has been directed elsewhere. The Victorians fixed on a realm beyond death, a place of transcendence, with their angels and crowns and doves. (It's often said of the Victorians that they were obsessed with death, but really they were in mass revolt against it: all those plumed horses, the crêpe, the marble, the silk gloves and parasols, the gleaming carriages heaped with flowers, were meant to sweeten the smell of decay.) Nowadays, attention is drawn back instead to a point before death, and our graveside imagery is more likely to feature a scene or token from the life now ended: photograph, flowerpot, pet cat, guitar.

The one place we do not encourage the eye to rest is on death itself, on the fearful object of the corpse. Fearful because it is paradoxical: abandoned by life but still bearing its resemblance, neither person nor non-person, precious but requiring disposal because it loses its wholesomeness so quickly. It's hard to imagine anyone choosing to mark a grave with a skull motif these days. It would seem morbid, inappropriate, in bad taste. Mourners at neighbouring graves would surely complain. It would not be allowed. Yet death itself has not once amended its customs or revised its protocols.

II

The graveyard at dawn. A slow disintegration, like the thawing of snow. Darkness melts in the same way here, particle by soft particle.

A Small Resurrection

Late one afternoon, when the trees have stopped dripping and the grass no longer glitters but stands full and sturdy with the day's rain, I'm following a route so familiar that I don't have to think about it but can let my mind wander freely and my feet find the direction. I'm approaching a handsome stone tomb where it's my custom to stop and read what's left of the inscription to Josiah Goodgame before continuing along the cinder path, through the lych-gate and home.

As I come close, I see that the tomb's surface is splashed with something – not rainwater, but something more substantial, something three-dimensional which seems to give off a faint green glow in the shade. My first thought is that this is some kind of chemical, spilt accidentally during an attempt to clean the stone, perhaps. Behind glass on a noticeboard by the outside tap there is a faded sheet of bullet-pointed instructions and prohibitions on the subject of cleaning gravestones: no wire wool, no bleach, no ammonia. Still, every now and then someone comes along and tries to erase the lichen with weedkiller or scour off the dirt with Domestos.

But no, this is not the result of a botched attempt to clean the stone. I recognise it now as nostoc, that curious substance which occasionally appears overnight on patios and garden paths, to be greeted either with fascination or horror depending on the temperament of the gardener. For the past four or five years it's been turning up intermittently in our small back garden in London, usually on an aluminium tabletop, which seems a surprisingly inhospitable choice of environment. Here it's scattered across the limestone surface of the tomb, lumps and gobbets of translucent goo among the blurred lettering. When I touch one with my finger, it's cold and viscid and slightly granular, a bit like stiff wallpaper paste.

It belongs to the phylum now called cyanobacteria, known until recently as blue-green algae: a category of micro-organisms with the ability to photosynthesise, and containing some of the earliest forms of life on earth. It has an ancient and noble lineage, this luminous gunk. But like frogspawn or cuckoo-spit, it's weird and repellent when first encountered; you're not sure for a moment whether it's plant, animal, or something other. Its unusual name was bestowed by the sixteenth-century scientist Paracelsus, and is probably a portmanteau of the Old English word *nosthryl* and its German equivalent, *Nasenloch*. I suppose it does bear a passing resemblance to snot, though so alarmingly copious that it would have to be from a monstrous or cosmic nosthryl; Paracelsus himself characterised it as 'pollution of some plethoricall and wanton Star, or rather excrement blown from the nostrils of some rheumatick planet'. As the description suggests, it was traditionally assumed to have fallen from the sky, either with rain or during a meteor shower, and its lexicon of folk-names testifies to its alien qualities: star-rot, troll's butter, astral jelly.

I look forward to the unscheduled appearances of our resident nostoc commune, but I suppose to the tidy gardener its arrival must be a great irritation. It's extremely difficult to get rid of. During dry weather it shrivels and dessicates, and lies dormant in the soil or in the cracks between paving slabs. It has the capacity to remain inert for long periods, near-invisible to the naked eye. It can survive hunkered down like this for months or even years, bursting into life after rainfall when everyone thought it was gone for good. There is at least one documented case in which a sample of nostoc was revived after being stored in a dry and apparently lifeless state in a museum for over a hundred years.

Here in the graveyard there is an abundance of places for it to hide out. Over the next few days, the gelatinous stuff I'm pushing with my fingertip will metamorphose, turn brown and crusty, and be scattered by the wind into the crevices between stones, among the moss and lichen, or in the ground on and around the graves, making itself so insignificant that it blends in and vanishes. It might find a habitat on the roots of plants, or between the gills of mushrooms. Then one day after rain – not next time, but maybe a month or even a year from now, unpredictably and according to some hidden prompting – it will be back again on Josiah Goodgame's tomb, like gooseberry jam dripped from a careless spoon all over the stone page.

I wonder what Josiah would have made of it. When I forget about jam and snot and wallpaper paste for a minute, look more carefully and refocus the image, nostoc takes on a different, more interesting kind of otherness. Its exceptional longevity, its extraordinary habit of going to ground and then manifesting as if from nowhere – these properties really should make it the most welcome of graveyard flora and fauna. *Love lives again, that with the dead has been*, reads the inscription on a neighbouring stone. You don't have to be a believer to feel there is something miraculous in the way this organism dies down and is resurrected again and again. In a graveyard we are often preoccupied with thoughts about the fragile and fleeting nature of life, but here is a reminder that life is also persistent, tenacious, regenerative. In the fading light, in this place where the dead have been, it glows with meaning like a living parable.

The Harkirk

'History offers the fantasy that it may be found; that out of all the
bits and pieces left behind, the past may be reconstructed, conjured
before the eyes: found.'

Carolyn Steedman, *Past Tenses: Essays on Writing,*
Autobiography and History

They said there was a secret graveyard at Crosby Hall. Each time
I passed the high perimeter wall of the estate, I wondered about
it. I noticed a small cross painted on the wall, and one day I
stopped and examined it, but I couldn't tell whether it signified
anything in particular. They said more than a hundred people
were buried there, although I once met someone who claimed that
her brother had sneaked in by a back way and searched all over
the grounds, and that he'd found no graveyard but did see the
ghost of the old gamekeeper, who raised his gun at him and then
vanished.

Now, following this meandering trail through my own past by
visiting my old places, I knew I had to see it for myself. I wrote a
letter – a good old-fashioned letter – to the lord of the manor,
requesting permission to visit. I wasn't entirely sure how to address
him, but he was a Blundell, and I knew the Blundells had been at
Crosby since the very beginning, so he would know all there was
to know about the graveyard. I felt faintly embarrassed, as if I were
proposing to go through the family jewellery. But a couple of days
later, a friendly email dropped into my inbox – he'd be delighted
to show me, just let him know when, yours, Mark.

The collision of then and now – the lord of the manor sitting down and dashing off an email – echoed throughout my journey here today. It's a journey I've made countless times before, driving back from elsewhere to my home just up the coast at Ainsdale, where I lived until a few years ago when my first marriage ended and I moved away. The route takes you north on the M62, joining the M57 where the motorway slices through what's left of the woods on the old estate at Halsnead Park, skimming past Knowsley Hall to the east, and then Croxteth Hall to the west, delivering you at the snarl of junctions known as Switch Island. Everything on that route is patched and written over and showing through. The past is stitched in with the present, the rural with the urban, wealth with impoverishment. Hunting lodge and colliery, deer-park and slum clearance, quarry and distribution centre. Then on through the Liverpool suburb of Great Crosby, where I turned off at the roundabout by the Sainsbury's superstore, past a straggle of 1930s semis, and out briefly into open fields to Little Crosby and the hall gates. When I drove in over the gravel and parked on the sweep, it was as though everything else had been wheeled off-stage – dual carriageway, street, retail park – revealing a completely different set. I paused for a moment looking up at the front of the house: pink sandstone, solid and pleasingly symmetrical, with a square turret at each corner. It seemed a tranquil and timeless view. Then Mark Blundell came to greet me and said, 'Of course it didn't always look like this – my parents had two-thirds of it pulled down in the fifties.'

Most graveyards are laid out and furnished for the living. They are maintained for the comfort and convenience of those who come to grieve, to pay their respects, learn about their ancestors, or retreat and be alone with their own thoughts. There may be gravel paths, a bench or two, a litter bin for the disposal of wilted flowers and cellophane wrappers, an outside tap and watering can.

The Harkirk has none of this. It's a secret place, enclosed and undisturbed by mourners. Birds know it, and foxes. A tiny chapel stands there, and a stone cross, but the high wall of the estate shields them from the road. When someone does find their way here, whether out of curiosity or by pure chance, they are met with stillness. The wind turns the pages of the trees, the sun drops sovereigns on the grass.

In 1611 a gruesome incident occurred near here. A woman died suddenly, and when her family approached the parson at the local parish church at Sefton he refused permission for her to be buried in the churchyard. They pleaded, but he would not give way. In desperation, they dug a shallow grave themselves, on a patch of common land next to the road. I imagine them working and grieving together, the son and the daughter, with whatever implements they had to hand. They did the best they could, but it was not good enough. Within days, pigs had rooted up the corpse and begun to devour it.

Interment in fields and gardens had become distressingly common in this part of Lancashire. It was the only way recusant families could bury their dead in this age of persecution. There was a weary irony in the situation: well within living memory, Protestants had been the ones demonised and scapegoated, but now the situation was reversed and it was the turn of Catholics to suffer. Those who would not conform were seen as subversives and extremists: the enemy within. Like other sectarian conflicts, it was a complex mix of politics, tribalism and religion – these elements are impossible to disentangle – but religious practice itself was the ground on which this battle was fought. Catholicism was now cast as heresy, and anyone discovered saying or singing mass was liable to heavy fines and imprisonment. The law compelled everyone to attend the parish church on Sundays and holy days, and those who refused were deemed guilty of recusancy. Since the Gunpowder Plot, and the wave of anger and fear that followed, the official line had hardened, and a crime which had been on the statute books for forty years was now brutally enforced. A special ecclesiastical council was set up in each district of England, with a remit to gather intelligence, reward informers and pass judgement on suspected persons. Once convicted, recusants were subject to severe restrictions on their movements and activities. They were not allowed to live within a certain radius of London, or to travel more than five miles from home without a special licence. They were debarred from holding public office, and from practising surgery, physic or law. It was an act of high treason for any seminary priest to enter England, or for anyone else to harbour or assist one.

Persecution did not end with death. According to the laws of the Church of England, recusants were automatically excommunicated. This meant spiritual banishment, and the loss of the privileges and protections that came with being part of a congregation. It also deprived them of their entitlement to burial in the consecrated ground of the churchyard: a kind of exile, which cut off access to traditional burial rites, excluded families from a sense of shared community, and crushed the expectation that they would be reunited with loved ones after death. In practice, there was room for individual clergymen to exercise a degree of discretion on the issue, but the parson at Sefton preferred to follow the rules scrupulously and without exception.

William Blundell, lord of the manor at Crosby, heard about the corpse desecrated by pigs. He was appalled, and decided the time had come to take action. '[It] were best to make readie in this village of Little Crosbie,' he wrote in his notebook, 'a place fitt to burie suche Catholiques either of myne owne howse or of the Neighbourhoode as should depte this lyfe duringe the tyme of these trobles.' If the church would not have them, he would make room for them on his own estate. The place he chose was a plot of land with a special history, said by local people to be the site where an ancient chapel once stood. It was known as the Harkirk, an Anglo-Saxon name meaning 'grey and hoary church', and although the church itself was a matter of legend by William Blundell's time, it lent all the right associations of sacredness and historical continuity. This piece of ground was consecrated by virtue of its past use, he decided, and would now become a holy and dignified place of burial for those refused it by the state.

When I pitched up in Ainsdale in my late twenties, I looked around me and thought I'd give it a year or two. Neither of us knew the area at all, but my husband needed to be here for a training placement. Like most of the places I've lived, this one was an accident of circumstance. It looked flat, grey and windswept. I stood on the doorstep with our baby daughter in my arms and said *It will do for now*.

There was never a moment when we decided to stay. That's just the way it went. We made friends, raised our children here, and survived a succession of career changes, redundancies and fresh starts. I walked back and forth over that same doorstep, in good times and hard times, for twenty years.

Neither of us could ever become a genuine local, known hereabouts as a Sandgrounder; to qualify, you must be born and bred on this 'ground of sand'. But we did gradually become part of a community. Not a community with common roots in place and religion, like the one at Little Crosby, but a web of connections, mostly with oddballs and blow-ins like ourselves. Then there were colleagues and neighbours, parents of our children's friends, teachers from their school, the people who ran the village show, the friendly couple in the fish shop, the milkman who was too shy to collect the money. It's community that makes a place home.

Mark Blundell leads me out through the back door of the hall, across the sunlit lawns and into the woods, bright with blown daffodils and scattered with brash left from a recent felling. They have an amazing machine which grips the trunk and slices it off, he tells me. It looks awful now, but in ten years it will all be worth it.

Managing an estate like this, you have to think long-term. Ten years is nothing.

It's hardly surprising that the boy who sneaked in looking for the graveyard couldn't find it. The boundaries of the burial ground are no longer delineated by William's original ditches and fences, and we have arrived before I realise it. The only thing which marks it out now is a series of deep trenches where archaeological excavations have taken place. Yes, says Mark, they did find a few bits and bobs. We climb a stile and make our way over the uneven ground to the stone cross. The shaft is modern, but the base is very ancient, and may even have marked the site of the original grey and hoary church. Close by is the tiny Victorian chapel, built in commemoration long after the burials had ceased and the danger passed.

There are no headstones marking the places of the dead. Just three pieces have survived. When the chapel was built, these three were salvaged and incorporated into the structure, forming part of the north wall. Two of them are dedicated to priests, and a little is known about both these men from diaries and records. The third, Jane Formby, has left virtually no trace except for this stone, with its pitted surface and incomplete lettering.

The chapel has wire grilles over the window, a wooden sign on the door asking respect for the place, and multiple locks. You can imagine we do have our problems here, says Mark, bringing out an enormous iron key. The locks have to be turned in a certain order and the door rocked and shoved in just the right way. I wonder how many months it is since it was last opened. For a minute or two it resists his efforts, then concedes with a heavy sigh.

A few of last year's leaves scuttle in after us, and halt abruptly as if disappointed by what they find. The interior is very plain, with whitewashed walls, benches and a simple altar made of slate. The only other feature is a tablet on the wall which lists all the burials that took place here. The names and dates have been transcribed from the register William began in 1611. There are 104 names listed in those early years. After a four-year hiatus starting in 1629, burials resume and continue until 1753, but on an occasional basis, and as a matter of choice rather than necessity.

The tablet in the chapel lists only the basic information, but the register itself, which I have examined in a storeroom at the British Museum, is meticulously detailed. The first entry, written in William Blundell's own hand, is an elderly man of the village:

> Ffirst of all, Wm Mathewson, an ould man of ye Morehowses within little Crosbie, dyed a Catholicke, the sixt daye of Aprill, anno Domini 1611, and was buried in ye Harkircke ye day following, being Sonday, and ye 7 day of Aprill aforesaid, being first denyed burial at Sephton Churche by the parson thereof.

The task of keeping the register was passed down through generations of Blundells, and the style of expression evolved along with the changing handwriting. The time of burial is often recorded, and the letter P added to denote a priest. As the years go on, the entries become longer and more biographical. Perhaps with time it was recognised that the register was not only a functional record but had commemorative value in itself. Perhaps it was envisaged that it might also serve as evidence of persecution, should this ever be needed. What began as a careful litany of names and dates begins to take on the colour and texture of lived experience. Edward Molyneux, a priest, was 'unfortunately killed by a faule off his horse'. John Nicholasson met his end 'coming from much Crosbie towne towards his owne hoesse the 27 day of December in the nighte, and being somewhat overseene with drinke (as it was thought) was drowned in a pitte'. A touching early description of dementia tells of the demise of Father George Lovell, 'a virtuous good Man and a very great Mathematission ... being become a perfect Child, and having entirely lost his Memory'.

On Jane Formby, the entry simply notes that she was servant to one of the priests in the hamlet of Carr Houses. I know the Jesuits had a safe-house there, with a chapel in the attic where mass could be held discreetly. I know where it stood, and I can imagine Jane walking the two miles there and back from the village to carry out her duties, across the fields and down the lane where I too have sometimes walked. I picture her as a girl, and then as an old woman. All her life she is a carrier of messages and a keeper of secrets. She comes from a family that has always kept the old faith, of course, and she's learned to be discreet, unobtrusive, utterly reliable. I see her walking the same route again and again, day in, day out: repetition to the point of ritual. There are the farmyard and barns which still stand today, though the safe-house is long gone. She is thinking as she walks. Things are not as bad as they were in her parents' day. But they say there will be another rebellion soon, and that means more fighting and killing, more children left without fathers. It's all so pointless and exhausting. What kind of God would sanction it? Ahead the lane narrows and peters out into a track leading to a small wood I know as Searchlight Plantation, though Jane would have called it by a different name. Then the flat, fertile land of the Moss, its miles of black fields criss-crossed with black ditches, under a vast ecumenical sky.

The creation and maintenance of a graveyard can be seen as one part of the contract between the living and the dead: a place for remembrance, in return for a sense of order and consolation. But the role of the burial place in providing facilities for the commemoration of each individual is quite a recent one. It seems to have taken hold around the time of the Industrial Revolution, and the mass migration of people away from their home villages to the cities where the work of manufacturing was concentrated. Families and communities were becoming less closely identified with particular places, and in the spacious new cemeteries that were being laid out in towns all over the country the individual grave began to assume greater significance.

Until then, the churchyard was the usual place of burial, and although some graves were marked with stones, they were the exception. Most bodies went into common graves. The individual was mourned, but the churchyard was not the focus of that mourning. What mattered most within its walls – and was enshrined as a legal right, though not a universal one – was for the dead to be gathered together, as they had been in life, and in a space consecrated for the purpose. To rest in holy ground, ready for the day of resurrection. To be remembered and honoured collectively, as members of a community that continued to hold meaning for those still living. These were among the claims and entitlements that were lost when the state disqualified some of its citizens from the churchyard. It was a dispossession.

In its own quiet and dignified way, the Harkirk was a piece of civil disobedience, and it got William Blundell into trouble. He was already a thorn in the side of the High Sheriff of Lancashire, Ralph Assheton. He had been arrested several times, and on other occasions forced into hiding. Now there was this new act of defiance. The burial ground may have been tucked away in the woods on the estate, but it wasn't long before official suspicions were roused. The parson at Sefton began to wonder what was happening to all the corpses he was turning away, and although the local population was overwhelmingly loyal to its squire, the king's pursuivants were everywhere, watching for signs of heresy, and well rewarded for the intelligence they gathered.

The Sheriff was determined to get William. In 1629 he sent his officers to Crosby Hall with a warrant to seize livestock as enforcement of unpaid fines for recusancy, but they met with resistance and had to turn back. William's own account paints a vivid picture of the confrontation: he writes of servants and villagers, 'weaponed with pykeforks, longstaves, and muchroukes', blocking the road and forcing the bailiffs to retreat.

Assheton was not about to give up. He and his men returned, this time armed with drawn swords. When their way was once more blocked, he began to take out his frustration on the locals.

'The Sherife meeting an ould woman above 64 yeares of age,' writes William,

> with a Pitchfork in her hand to take upp a boate of flaxe out of the reeting place as she tould him, he commanded her to lay it downe ... then shee went on her waye upp the lane, and the Sherife ridde after her, and overtaking her brooke her head with the pumell of his swoard that the bloud ranne downe her face, whereupon shee gave him foule words ... and setting the point of his naked swoarde to her brest, swore hee would sticke her.

In the course of this gratuitously violent encounter, Assheton insults the old woman by addressing her as 'Demdike'. She must surely have recognised this epithet as the nickname of Elizabeth Southerns, one of the accused at the Pendle witch-trials a decade earlier, and herself a notorious recusant. He is not just calling the woman a witch, but conflating witchcraft with Catholicism, in a demonstration of just how crude and bitter the animosity had become.

When the bailiffs returned with their warrant once more, and were again seen off by a ragtag army of locals armed with agricultural tools, it was the last straw. William Blundell was summoned to appear before the Star Chamber. He was accused of two offences: first of inciting a riot, and second, 'that he did take & enclose a little parcell of ground in Little Crosbie aforesaid ... and caused the same to bee walled about with stone in the forme & manner of a Churche yard ... & caused the sayd piece of ground to be hallowed and consecrated for a place to burie the dead in by popishe priests and jesuitts'. He was convicted, and fined the enormous sum of £2,000.

The order was given for the destruction of the Harkirk. According to an account written by William's daughter Margaret, the Sheriff and thirty of his men 'pulled down the walls, knocking the stone to pieces ... and carried away the crosses with much derision, having also dug up some part of the graves. All this was done with the sound of trumpet, they both coming and going away with great pomp'.

*

A wood can be a good place to encounter fragments of the past. Not the kind of wood which is managed for shooting or logging, or provides sylvan paths and picnic benches, but the kind no one cares too much about, which is neither productive nor attractive to walkers. There may not be a sign saying *Keep Out*, but still, you can't be sure it's safe to enter. You wonder whether you're being watched. Stepping into a wood like that, you cross a threshold between *now* and *then*. Whatever was once installed, concealed or abandoned may still be there, hidden in the undergrowth, waiting for you to chance across it.

There is nothing left of the wartime searchlight battery in Searchlight Plantation, but in nearby Tower Wood it is possible to see large chunks of ornamental masonry lying like broken gravestones, scattered and mossy, though the tower that gave the place its name has passed into legend. The local woods – Crow Wood, Flea Moss Wood, Waterhen Clump, Trap Plantation – have the feel of edgelands about them, scruffy and ignored, dusty and vibrating with the traffic on the A565. I have never heard their names spoken, but the map remembers them. Then there's Sniggery Wood. Its name was a tantalising mystery to me for years, until I stumbled across it in the *Great Diurnal*, a series of diaries kept by William Blundell's great-grandson Nicholas in the eighteenth century. There I learned that 'snig' is an old word for eel, and a sniggery was an eel fishery. There would have been traps here, and a shelter for the fishermen. There is no sign of those now, but the pools and ditches remain.

In the managed woods of the Blundell estate, on the site of the unofficial graveyard where 131 men, women and children were buried, the few surviving relics have been carefully preserved: just these three small headstones, all of them from the Harkirk's later phase. The Sheriff's men must have done a thorough job in 1629; the Star Chamber trial heard witness statements which described 'faire gravestones ... with letters and figures thereupon engraved as monuments or remembrances', but no piece of any of these has been found.

For William Blundell, the forgotten past was brought dramatically to light with the digging of the very first grave, for old Mr Mathewson. Early the next morning, a servant boy was driving cattle from the house to a field close to the burial place when he spotted something on the displaced earth, glinting in the April sunshine. 'Hee sawe upon the sandie coppe caste within the sayde place certayne peeces of Coyne scattered (as it seemed) with the throwinge of them with the sand owte of the ditch', wrote William. 'Seekinge and scrapinge in the sandie Coppe, wee founde a number more before dinner.' Later the same day, he returned with his wife, brother and son, and found yet more. 'In all, there were fownde at one tyme and other above fower schore pieces, none bigger than a groate, and none less than a twoe pence.'

The discovery of the ancient coins was miraculous in William's eyes. He had stayed true to his principles, putting himself and his family in danger by creating this burial ground. It was a considerable personal risk, taken purely for reasons of conscience. And the digging of the very first grave yielded hidden treasure! This could not be a coincidence, he thought. It was a gift from heaven, and it brought with it certain obligations. It must be used in the right way. According to the law of the land, he was required to relinquish most of it, as treasure trove found hidden in the earth was owed to the Crown. But he chose instead to refer to a later source which provided a legal exception to the usual rule. According to this rubric, silver found in a churchyard was a special case and should be treated differently. It should be divided into two, one half belonging to the Crown and the other to the Church. Here was a way of asserting the moral authority of his project, he decided. So in an act of religious defiance, he had a quantity of the coins melted down and made into a chalice and a pyx. The chalice was stolen in the nineteenth century, but the pyx is kept at the British Museum. It looks a bit like an old-fashioned watch case, surprisingly dull and dark for silver, and is engraved with the inscription: *This was made of silver found in the burial place W Bl.*

William became fascinated with his hoard of coins, studying them closely, researching their history and presenting his conclusions in an essay. He argues that the hoard – which included coinage of the Saxon kings Alfred the Great and Edward the Elder, and of the Danish king Cnut of Northumbria – was deposited by the Danes during their confrontation with the Hiberno-Norse forces in the tenth century. The reading and thinking he did on the subject strengthened his conviction that he had chosen the right place for his burial ground, and that it had indeed been the site of an ancient church, as villagers claimed. During turbulent times, when a place was sought to conceal money and valuables, a church-yard was considered a wise choice. The ground was already disturbed, so that signs of fresh digging might go unnoticed; and there was some chance that holy ground would be left alone, so that whatever was hidden there would stay put. Of course, the intention was to come back when peace and order had returned, and retrieve the hidden possessions. But if the owner was killed, the secret died with him.

Buried secrets can stay safe for a very long time, but once they are dug up and brought into the light they are instantly at risk. In the refuge of the ground, under the lid of turf, the coins had lain together and undisturbed for 600 years. But only 30 years after they were unearthed by the gravedigger, when the threat of civil war loomed ever closer, they were packed up and sent away to relatives in Wrexham for safekeeping, where they were mysteriously lost. William's meticulous pen-and-ink drawings of them survive, but the coins themselves have vanished. Perhaps they were stashed away somewhere by a conscientious cousin, and are still there, waiting to be rediscovered all over again.

The body of Edward Molyneux, the priest who died falling from his horse in 1704, was brought to the Harkirk from the beach at

Formby, where it had been discovered by a fisherman. His death was a puzzle to some – he was an experienced horseman, and in robust good health – but others were not surprised. Suspicion immediately fell on Old Trash, a great black dog who had borne the blame for many deaths over the generations. He was recognisable by his red eyes and by the way he splashed through the waterlogged sand without leaving any prints. He must have crossed Father Edward's path as he rode home along the beach. Everyone knew that to set eyes on Old Trash was to be cursed, instantly and irreversibly.

Many years later, a man awaiting execution for another crime made a spontaneous confession. He admitted that during his time as an ostler at a Liverpool inn, he had tricked a priest who stopped to rest and dine there. He swapped the priest's fleet horse for another, slower one, then waited for him to set off home, mounted the good horse himself and galloped after him. He overtook him on the lonely sands, dragged him violently to the ground with the intention of robbing him, but then realised he had killed him, took fright and fled empty-handed. By unburdening his conscience, he cleared up an old mystery at last. Nevertheless, some minds were not changed; there were those who continued to believe that Old Trash must have played a part, somehow.

Superstition and legend offer ways of making sense of death and trauma, when the usual ways fail us. Close to Carr Houses, where the Jesuits had their safe-house, a ghost known as the Grey Lady has often been seen to dart out from Cross Barn Lane into the main road at night. The lane is a quiet byway, leading to an ancient cruck-framed barn in the shape of a cross, where recusants met for mass during the time of their persecution; it has been suggested that the Grey Lady is fleeing the scene when she dashes into the path of the traffic. The place where these sightings occur is an accident blackspot, and even today she is occasionally cited as a possible cause when a car collides with an oncoming lorry or careers off into a ditch. It is an unnerving route to drive late at night. The road suddenly narrows and passes through a belt of dark woodland. Strange structures loom up out of nowhere: on one side a circular house with a tall chimney, on the other a baroque gateway guarded by stone lions. The car headlights pick out flashes of water from obscure pools between the trees, never seen in daytime, and, every now and then, a bunch of flowers taped to a tree-trunk. I don't believe in ghosts, but if I ever see one it could well happen here.

Of course the truth is that there has never been any shortage of things to die from. Childbirth, accident, famine, a multitude of infectious diseases. During the Harkirk years, the towns and villages of Lancashire suffered recurring outbreaks of plague, smallpox, typhus and ague, and it was probably one of these which led to the spate of infant burials recorded in the register in the spring of 1621. On 22 May, a mass grave was dug, and William wrote: 'In this space were buried 2 Infants of Thomas Blundell of ye Morehowses, 1 of Thomas Holmes of Douholland, 2 of Richarde Bryanson's of ye Morehowse, 1 of Richard Marrowe's of little Crosbie, viz. 6.'

Last night I dreamt about lost things again. All the searching and researching I've been doing at Crosby is creating echoes in my dreams. This time I was approaching our old house – the one where I lived for twenty years – but however hard I tried I could never reach the front door. I was aware I'd forgotten something or left something behind. There was no hoard of coins, of course, secreted away for the duration of the war. But there seemed to be something else of value, hidden in the garden or under the floorboards. Perhaps the earring with the turquoise stone, one of a pair bought on honeymoon, and mourned a decade later? Or the skeletons of pet rabbits and goldfish and mice; I could still recite the names the children gave them, though they were legion. The cork from the bottle of champagne we opened on a birthday or anniversary. The bulbs of crocus and snowdrop and narcissus, bought autumn after autumn in a spirit of optimism and buried guiltily, sometimes much too late, when they had gone soft in the paper bag. A child's shoelace. A nappy pin. Sand, trodden everywhere from our walks on the beach. My hand was on the gate, and I could feel the blistered paint and the cold metal underneath. The time of strife is long over, the dream told me, it's time to go back and retrieve the treasure.

Retrieve, from the Old French *retrover*, to find again. To go back and recover what has been lost: surely one of the most influential of human impulses. It has us digging and metal-detecting, reading inscriptions, trawling through archives, revisiting old haunts, poring over photograph albums, tracking down schoolfriends and ex-lovers we didn't like all that much in the first place. We talk of retrieving memories too, as if they were coins stashed away for safe-keeping. As if the past were a drawer that could be wrenched open, creaking and jamming, and its contents rummaged for valuables. If only we remember hard enough, perhaps we can get back the thing, the place, the person we left behind. Perhaps we can even recover our earlier selves. The historian Carolyn Steedman describes 'the hope that that which is gone, that which is irretrievably lost, which is past time, can be brought back, and conjured before the eyes "as it really was"; and that it can be possessed'. The impulse to retrieve is a longing to outwit time. To defeat death itself.

Any act of retrieval here at the Harkirk could only ever be partial. When the thirty men came and smashed up the graveyard, they must have hoped to cancel the possibility altogether. They confiscated the crosses which marked the burial places, and perhaps also the tall stone cross which had stood there for centuries. There must be no community of the recusant dead – not in the churchyard, not anywhere. No opportunity for commemoration by the living. Like the deliberate destruction of cemeteries in time of war and ethnic cleansing, this was a symbolic act of obliteration.

The massive iron key turns the lock on the chapel and its list of names. We scuff through the last of the old leaves to take another look at the three old headstones. They all date back to Nicholas

Blundell's time, and two of them feature in his *Great Diurnal*. They were both priests: John Layton, whose sermons were said to draw such large congregations it was difficult to find a barn large enough to accommodate them; and Robert Aldred, Nicholas's favourite, 'a Laborious good Missionor, a Fasatious plesant man, and very well beloved by Protestants as well as Catholicks'.

The third, Jane Formby, is not mentioned. She probably made little impression on the squire, given that she was both a woman and a servant. Besides, he is preoccupied with other pressing matters. By the time of her death, persecution had begun to loosen its grip, but sectarian division and distrust was still a reality. The Jacobite uprisings brought riots and skirmishes to nearby towns, and it seems Nicholas Blundell sheltered a fugitive rebel at the hall for a time. Nicholas was a peaceable man who cultivated social contacts on both sides of the religious divide, but this was a tense time for him. He writes of a series of official intrusions, with soldiers searching the estate for horses, weapons and gunpowder. There were a few secret hiding places in the house – a false roof, a gap between walls – which were intended for visiting priests. But on at least one occasion he had to conceal himself, an experience he records with the laconic entry: 'Nov. 16th. I set in a Streat place for a fat Man'.

Jane herself would be entirely forgotten were it not for the note in the burial register, and the piece of stone carved with her name. A hundred and fifty years later, when the workmen came to build the memorial chapel and unearthed this fragment as they dug the footings, they must have wondered about her too. The squire gave instructions for it to be brushed clean and heaved into place alongside the two others in the wall of the chapel. It was then more than a century since the last burial, and the Harkirk was once again a green and tranquil place, disturbed only by foxes and deer. Its role in sheltering the dead had long passed out of living memory, and even in the village the story was not well known. The new chapel would restore that piece of history, and with it a sense of family pride in what had been done by William and his successors.

This place is not really about Jane Formby, or Robert Aldred, or John Layton. The three carved stones act as representatives. The burial register names each individual, makes each one real and singular, but what mattered even more was the continuation of a community, not just in life but in death too. In the Christian tradition of the time, the most important service the dead performed for the living was intercession for the forgiveness of their sins and the salvation of their eternal souls. But by lying together in this dedicated place they fulfilled other functions too: reinforcing a sense of identity and belonging, reminding those still living of the dark times of persecution, and cautioning future generations against complacency and the risk it might happen again.

Jane Formby is no relative of mine, and she died nearly 300 years ago. Why come and look at her name on a stone as if I could retrieve her? There's nothing left to know. I don't live here any more, and none of this has anything to do with me. I'm already checking my watch, preparing to walk away and get in my car and drive back into the present tense.

Still, I think, running my finger along the lines of the inscription, someone took a hammer and chisel and worked her name on a stone. Someone dipped the pen into ink and wrote it in the register. Someone wept at the graveside, quietly, and under cover of night.

III

The drowned graveyard. When the last trump sounded, the North Sea took the dead: the coffins with their lead linings and brass handles, the railing and the fancy gravel, the vanished names — Septimus, Ebenezer, Chastity — the *here lieth*, the *perished in infancy*, the *relict thereof*, the *mouldiring frame of clay*, the buried prayer-book and wedding ring, the wigs and slippers, the broken locket, the *late lamented* and the unlamented, the angels with their ivied faces, the urn, the rose-bowl and the silk carnation, yea all the chattels of the dead, and also their park and purlieus, all yielded at last to the judgement of the deep, and dispersal to its different addresses.

Forever

'The mason stirs:
Words!
Pens are too light.
Take a chisel to write.'

Basil Bunting, *Briggflatts* (Part 1)

The surface of this headstone is breaking up into large, thin flakes, peeling away and exposing the softer layer beneath. In the damp fissure between the two, black mould has found lodging. The texture of the spalling stone is so unusual that I can't resist reaching out and touching it lightly with my fingertips, and to my horror the phrase *Loving Memory* falls off in one piece onto the grass.

Sandstone is particularly prone to this kind of weathering, where moisture seeps between the layers: either rising, wicked up from the earth beneath like drink through a straw, or hurled at the face of the stone as rain, freighted with windborne salt or acid. Sometimes the entire surface is sloughed as a single sheet, the stone underneath still bearing the shape of the letters and images carved through from above. A bad case of spalling can erase the inscription entirely, like an attack of total amnesia.

For the bereaved, death makes a tear in the fabric of self. It can be difficult to accept that it has really happened, difficult even to retain that knowledge from one day to the next. For a time after my mother's death, I would wake up morning after morning and take myself through the painful remembering, again and again. Here was a piece of knowledge so momentous that it had to be learned repeatedly before it could be assimilated. The waking and remembering was accompanied not only by sorrow but also by incredulity. To believe that the vibrant person I knew so well was gone was to understand that this is a world in which *anything* can happen. Even my own immortality was called into question.

Eventually, of course, we do learn, because we are not inflexible, it just takes time. The hole in the fabric is not repaired, but we go on living with it in its damaged condition. It's in our nature, after an interval, to turn back to our own lives, however changed we are by our loss. A stone memorial speaks of this ambivalence: erected once the first blaze of grief has begun to subside, its office is to stand solid and unchanging even as the bereaved adapt and move on. When it comes to marking the place of burial, wood, brick and metal have all been pressed into service, but stone is the favourite: hard, enduring, abundant stone, which can be cut and carved and has a weight and solidity that says *We will not forget*.

When there was a death in a small village, everyone knew about it. But with mass migration from village to city, the old assumptions didn't hold true. In a city, there were deaths every day. Here, a person could live unknown and die unnoticed, even by neighbours in the same district. In response to this bewildering new reality, the memorial became more important and, for those who could afford it, more elaborate. It announced and recorded the loss; it was a way of keeping the memory alive, of fixing it in a place which would otherwise all too quickly forget. It was a statement of belonging, and an affirmation of individual significance. The city was always restless, shifting, reinventing itself, and a stone represented stillness and permanence. To publish a person's name and dates there was a bid for posterity. The life might be extinguished, but the firmness of stone, and the work of the mason's chisel, would testify forever that they had lived.

But forever is far too long. None of these stones is immune to the effects of weather, and the afflictions of old age. They decline, as we do. Some develop large blisters, which give off a hollow sound if tapped with a fingernail. Others grow stubbly, pitted and scarred. Lichens and algae colonise cracks and crevices too small to see with the naked eye, multiplying and spreading over limestone in kaleidoscopic forms. Words blur and lose their definition, or the stone recedes and the leading stands proud on its pegs like long teeth before loosening and falling out.

The visible dead crowd this place, with their headstones and angels, their kerb-sets and vases, all the paraphernalia of memorial. But the dead I can count are vastly outnumbered by those I can't; the earth beneath holds the bones of thousands more, most laid in mass graves, marked in a temporary way or not at all. Then there are the new graves, still in their 'settling' period: the earth shifting and stabilising, and a small wooden cross marking the place. Some will never acquire a headstone. The wooden cross will remain, until it is broken or blown away in the wind.

Where relatives or friends have gone to the trouble and expense of engraving a stone, it may be read less often than they hope. To begin with, the intention is to make regular pilgrimage, to brush the stone clean, keep the weeds down, lay flowers. But in time the living resume their lives, and the routines of maintenance tend to be abandoned. After fifteen years, very few graves are visited at all.

Before the Industrial Revolution, memorials were made of stone sourced locally, and there were regional variations which lent each historic churchyard its own character. There were some exceptions: foreign stone might be shipped for a special piece, and before the Fens were drained in the seventeenth century stone quarried in the Midlands was brought by raft along its network of channels to remote parishes where the local alternatives were limited. Later, with the coming of new transport links – first the canal, then the railway – came the mass import of exotic stone: limestone into northerly areas, sandstone to the south and east, Italian marble for those who could afford it. With customer choice, fashions came and went, and the distinctive local character of the churchyard was gradually relinquished.

These days, it's a global business. The most common choice everywhere now is polished black granite, quarried in India, China and South Africa and shipped all over the world. At a glance, it all looks the same, but there are many varieties, some more highly prized than others for the fineness of the grain and the consistency of colour, which make for high-contrast engraving and sharper lettering. Some are not true granites but dolerites, gabbros and basalts, sold under names like Shanxi Black, Jet Black and Zoom Black. But in a fiercely competitive market, they all deliver what the customer seems to want: a shiny, modern, weather-resistant product which looks everlasting.

Polished granite is an ideal medium for the new methods of production. Modern memorials are shaped by machine. The inscription, once the preserve of highly skilled craftsmen working with hammer and chisel, or by a process of stencilling and sand-blasting, is now a matter of manipulating text and images on computer and sending the file to a laser engraving machine. '*Design your headstone in 4 easy steps!*' reads the banner headline on one website. The customer uploads the words, and chooses from a bank of stylised images – teddy bear, cherub, dove, rose – then the graphic designer loads the artwork, and the machine does the rest. Portrait photographs, long a feature of cemeteries in mainland Europe, are now part of the funerary landscape here too.

Rows and rows of black granite, mass-produced in a limited range of designs and polished to a high-gloss finish, give the new area of a cemetery a strangely high-tech appearance, as if it had been furnished with rows of giant smartphones. And perhaps this outlandish image is not so wide of the mark, since it is now possible to erect a 'living headstone' with a QR code embedded in a plastic tag, so that the visitor can scan it and be taken to a webpage containing information about the deceased.

In the old churchyard, I hurry guiltily away from the scene of my accidental vandalism, leaving the spalling stone and the wafer of text on the grass, and retracing my careful steps through a junkyard of brambles and broken monuments. If fifteen years is the best we can hope for, we might as well go back to marking graves with soft local varieties, or even wood. But it's granite people go for: a material which will last 200 years or more, machine-engraved and laser-etched to be read by generations yet to be born. This is the paradox at the heart of our human efforts to remember and memorialise: the wish to last forever, and the knowledge that we are doomed to fail.

Rapparee

'Cawk! cawk! the crew and skipper
Are wallowing in the sea:
So there's a savoury supper
For my old dame and me.'

Rev. R. S. Hawker, 'A Croon on Hennacliff'

The organist has locked himself in, and is practising the same three hymn tunes over and over. A woman with a box full of papers is thumping the heavy old door and rattling the handle, but he doesn't hear her over the music. The cycle repeats and repeats. He returns now to the George Herbert hymn 'Teach Me, My God and King', though it's a simple tune and I'm surprised he needs to go over it so often. Perhaps he's just playing for the pleasure of it.

The church is on a hill above the seaside town of Ilfracombe, beyond range of the sounds of its fish-and-chip cafés, crazy golf and amusement arcades. It's high summer, and the graves are deep in flowering grasses, poppies, red campion, ox-eye daisies. Through a gap in the hedge, a modern extension stretches away across the valley towards the Torrs and the sea: its grass cut short, paths neatly trimmed. Floral tributes wilt in the heat. Their cellophane wrappings glitter like small mirages. Three hymns on a repeating loop, and the cries of seagulls, and the drone of a lawnmower, somewhere just out of sight.

A man that looks on glass, / On it may stay his eye; / Or if he pleaseth, through it pass, / And then the heav'n espy. When I think of those lines, I remember the tall windows of the chapel I attended as a child. They were made of bubbled glass which altered the view. As I sat through the long sermon, sucking the coin I had been given to put on the collection plate, I would look up at those windows for a glimpse of the outdoors, a shiver of bird or tree moving in the wind, made mysterious by the glass. I would sit and watch, with the blood taste of the coin in my mouth, idly noticing the way things were, and the way things seemed to be, and the space between.

The air is forgetful with pollen, the bees are drunk in the fox-gloves. Too many graves, too many dead to reckon. The next tune starts up. I wander on, sneezing and reading the inscriptions, no-ticing how many drownings there are. Scores of them. Fishermen, lifeboatmen, schoolchildren, holidaymakers, drinkers returning from inns, lovers returning from trysts. Mariners from Italy, France, Norway, Greece, but mostly local men, killed in the course of a day's work. The sea, like the cholera, has a tendency to devour whole families. The Buckinghams, for instance, lost James in 1853, Edmund in 1858, Henry in 1861, and Charles in 1887. And when a ship went down, the loss was often total: a stone marks the mass grave of six men, the captain and crew of the brig *Wilberforce*, wrecked in 1842.

When he visited in 1722, Daniel Defoe observed 'a good mar-ket and port town, called Ilfar-Comb, a town of good trade, populous and rich, all which is owing to its having a very good harbour and road for ships'. The sea shapes and defines everything: work and leisure, fortune and the loss of it, local character, sense of self. I began to understand this vividly soon after coming to live here. I was twenty-four and newly married, about to take up my first teaching job in a nearby village school, my pupils the children of farmers and owners of holiday bed-and-breakfasts and camp-sites. I knew no one. We came because we had fallen in love with the place on a field trip the previous summer; back then, it was as easy as that. For the first six months we lived in a flat, cheap but eccentrically furnished – black bathroom, black carpets, black plastic sofa – a few minutes' walk from the churchyard in one direction, the sea in the other. I had grown up in a landlocked Midlands town, and I was surprised to find this place not just *by* the sea, but *of* it. There was no corner of any street where you could escape from the sound of the gulls, or the taste of salt on your lips. Here you could smell a storm coming in, or watch a high tide vault the sea wall and race across the street. Homes and livelihoods, reputations and relationships were built and staked and lost on the strength of those tides.

This town has always faced the elements squarely, dealt with them, profited as best it can. Here between the drowned is the grave of a man who knew those elements well but died peacefully in his bed at the age of 85. He too had made the sea his living, not on a fishing boat or clipper but by smuggling and wrecking. This drowsy spot, and the modest stone which marks it, seems an unlikely destination for Hanibal Richards, sometime leader of a notorious gang which for decades controlled the nearby village of Lee.

In the collective imagination the smuggler is usually cast as a lovable rogue, a reckless man of action with his own peculiar code of honour. He uses natural cunning and local knowledge to outwit the authorities, contributing to the redistribution of wealth in the process. The spoils are shared, and the hard times eased by them. Constables and clergymen turn a blind eye; customs men are bought off, or stonewalled; there's brandy for everyone, and no questions asked.

In 1789, Hanibal Richards moved to Lee from the village of Morwenstow, just over the border in Cornwall. He brought with him a set of special skills learned during his time as a member of the legendary smuggling and wrecking outfit known as Coppinger's Gang. The gang's leader, whose ruthlessness earned him the epithet 'Cruel' Coppinger, is a cryptic figure, said to have wrought havoc from a clifftop cottage at Welcombe, where a shard of old window-glass on which he scratched his name is still kept in a kitchen drawer. But navigating the line between fact and fiction is like getting lost in a sea mist. The legend tells that Coppinger was a giant, either Danish or Irish, the only survivor of a shipwreck in a great storm. He strides semi-naked out of the sea and seizes a local maiden and her horse, galloping off with both to her father's house, where he installs himself and bewitches the girl into marriage. Then he summons his gang to join him, and converts the family home into his criminal headquarters. He acquires a ship called the *Black Prince*. There are drownings and beheadings. He bullies his father-in-law into an early grave, and extorts money from his mother-in-law by torturing her daughter. There is a curse, a miraculous thunderbolt, a son born without a soul. And then finally he leaves, the same way he arrived: a mysterious ship looms up out of the storm one night, and he leaps aboard, never to be seen again.

The Coppinger legends were collected by the Reverend Hawker of Morwenstow, who was well-known for his love of a good story. His accounts of life and death on the Cornish coast are a mare's nest of first-hand experience, oral history, village gossip and fantasy. But there's no doubt he understood the ways in which an armed gang could bring terror to a small community. Mobs and effigies. Blackmail, kidnapping, punishment beating.

We can't know how the real Coppinger measured up against his legendary counterpart, and Hanibal Richards is more enigmatic still. With only a few shreds of local mythology to go on, it's impossible to judge what kind of man he was. No magic powers are attributed to him, and there is no suggestion that he carried off any virgins. He was a smuggler of some notoriety, but 'smuggling' is a slippery word that resists easy definitions. Things are made more ambiguous still by its inscrutable relationship with 'wrecking'; indeed, wrecking itself has a double meaning which casts it in different degrees of shadow. The ransacking of shipwrecks for their cargo was as old and enduring an occupation as seafaring itself, and had persisted despite official attempts to control it. Among poor people living on the coast, it was regarded as a kind of harvest, and most of the time there was no obvious victim; if anyone lost out, it was the shipping cartels or the insurance companies, and no one was inclined to feel guilty on their account. It wasn't always so straightforward, however. The wild and inaccessible coast around Lee and the village of Mortehoe to the south has seen countless wrecks. The *Wilberforce*, whose crew lie in that mass grave I saw just now, was one casualty among many, broken to pieces on the rocks in dense fog. But a little while after the event, a rumour began to circulate that the *Wilberforce* had been deliberately lured to catastrophe by smugglers showing a false light.

A retired clergyman, the Reverend Charles Crump, was scandalised by stories like this one, and began a campaign to improve safety at sea. Like many a cause, it was advanced first by means of a poem, published and distributed at his own expense. It's no work of literature, but it is remarkable for its sustained pitch of righteous anger. It denounces the local wreckers, characterising them as 'the vampires of Morte Bay'. Crump reserves his greatest fury for one vampire in particular:

> Have ye ne'er heard men tell, the fiendish deed,
> Of that feel woman, who, from cursed greed
> Of plunder, merged beneath the whelming tide
> A shipwrecked mariner, who struggling died
> Under her iron prongs? And know ye not
> Of that fierce murd'ress, the fearful lot?

He names no names, but he must surely have had in mind Elizabeth Berry, a Mortehoe woman with an atrocious reputation for getting her hands on the loot regardless of the human cost. The law did not allow anyone to claim salvage from a shipwreck if there were any survivors, and Elizabeth was notorious for her willingness to overcome this legal obstacle, finishing off exhausted sailors by holding them underwater with a pitchfork until they drowned.

I hoped I might find Elizabeth Berry's grave here in the church-yard, but now I see it would be an impossible task, like turning up in a city you don't know and hoping to bump into someone you've only met once. Though such chance meetings can and do happen: I stand for a few minutes staring at the name John Phillips Chiswell, before it comes into focus in my memory: he was a pilot and life-boatman in the late eighteenth and early nineteenth centuries whose reminiscences I was reading in the town museum just this morning.

It's unlikely that any memorial would mark Elizabeth's grave anyway, since her family seem to have been desperately poor. One foggy morning, according to the record, she was arrested on a cliff path, on her way back from the beach where a fishing boat had come to grief with all hands lost. She was dragging behind her a sack of stolen goods which were found to comprise a tub and a bed-sack. There's no mention of the pitchfork on this occasion, and the spoils seem pitiful. She could not pay the fine of £1, and the magistrate sent her to prison 'to warn her and others against such dastardly conduct, in taking away from the unfortunate mariners, especially those lying dead on the shore, any part of their property'.

Every gift shop in the West Country sells books of smugglers' tales, and every seaside town has its Smuggler's Inn. It's the myth-kitty of this region, an essential part of its sense of identity, and a source of harmless if hackneyed fun for the grockles. But occasionally something happens which brings the past spilling out into the present, and changes the mood completely.

In 1997, the buried past made a dramatic reappearance on one of Ilfracombe's beaches. The sea itself did the work. Storms had eroded the base of the cliff, and when a high tide breached a retaining wall a quantity of very old bones tumbled out onto the sand. Pieces of iron were found among them which might have been fetters.

The site of the discovery is Rapparee Cove, a narrow inlet sheltered by jagged rocks. I remember standing at the harbour wall
with binoculars one afternoon in 1986, and looking across the
water to Rapparee. I knew it had been a Victorian bathing beach,
because occasionally you could turn up old postcards in the junk
shop with black-and-white photographs featuring the row of
beach huts, bathing machines and refreshment kiosk. I have one
which shows the tiny Rapparee Ferry being rowed ashore bearing
half a dozen ladies with hats and parasols. These were the images
I had in my mind as I focused the binoculars beyond the glittering
masts of the harbour, onto the black rocks which shattered the
waves and flung them over the ashy sand. It was summer. I had an
ice-cream in my other hand. I had no idea I was looking at the site
of a mass grave.

A decade later, when the wall burst open at the back of the
beach, it was as though a hole was breached in the collective memory and some long-forgotten things fell out along with the bones.
The first was the recollection that a schoolboy, playing truant at
Rapparee in the '60s, had gone home with a coin in his hand:
Portuguese gold, dated 1725. At the time, this find had itself stirred
the mud of the past, reminding older townspeople that similar
coins had been found in their own childhood days, whenever
storms had disturbed the sand and revealed them. Word of the boy
and his find got around, sparking a miniature gold-rush, when the
little beach was thronged with treasure-hunters bringing spades
and metal detectors.

Next, thoughts turned to the strange yellow stones which could
be seen on the sand from time to time, and which according to
legend were remnants of the ballast from a ship wrecked there on
its way back from the West Indies.

And then, further back, there was the memory of a memory,
handed down from parents and grandparents, about a scandal in
the local press: a fiery exchange in the nineteenth century between
two correspondents, in the course of which the people of Ilfracombe

were condemned as wreckers and smugglers and accused of an appalling crime.

Pat Barrow, local man and amateur archaeologist, had been obsessed with Rapparee Cove most of his adult life, and the bones came as no surprise to him. He had long suspected that there were bodies buried there, and that they, along with the gold coins and the yellow stones, came from an Admiralty transport ship called the *London*, wrecked here in 1796. His research suggested that more than sixty people had drowned in the disaster, and that only some of the bodies were carried up the hill to the churchyard for burial. Others, he understood, were buried on the beach, right next to the place where the striped deckchairs and beach huts were installed a hundred years later.

When the retaining wall collapsed, and the evidence fell out onto the sand, Pat pieced together what was known about the *London*. He obtained permission to carry out an excavation of the site, which yielded many more bones and teeth. He matched up eyewitness accounts and Admiralty records. But when he talked about his findings, he was taken aback by the hostility they provoked. It seemed that the events of 1796 could still cause shock and outrage 200 years later. He found himself at the centre of a media storm, and for a time engulfed by it: attempting to steer the right course between violently opposing views on the fate of the ship and, crucially, the status of the people who drowned.

One way of dealing with a painful experience, and the internal conflict it generates, is to forget it. But collective forgetting is not easy, and it can never be decisive. Whatever is buried will eventually work its way to the surface. Ilfracombe was used to shipwrecks, but this was not just any shipwreck. The records show that the *London* was carrying the spoils of war: not only gold coins but also a large number of prisoners, captured during fighting on the island of St Lucia, one of the battlegrounds in the early years of the Napoleonic Wars. The British forces had defeated the French and seized control of the island, which was of great strategic importance. During their occupation, the French had enslaved the local population, and when the island was attacked these slaves were enlisted to fight in its defence, with the promise of freedom in return. Two thousand St Lucians staged a brave last stand against the British forces at Fort Charlotte, but the battle went against them and all were either killed or forced to surrender. The prisoners, wounded and exhausted, were marched aboard the *London* and chained below deck for the long voyage to Bristol. It is not clear what future was envisaged for them once they arrived, or whether the captain of the ship had his own plans. The campaign against the slave trade was well underway, and public opinion was turning against it, but abolition was more than a decade away, and there were still profits to be made.

It was the word 'slaves' which sent shockwaves through the town, and beyond. Some sources insisted on identifying the men only as prisoners of war, but it's a difficult semantic position to defend in the face of the evidence: records from Bristol where the survivors were taken list them explicitly as 'Mulatto Slaves' and 'Negro Slaves'. The records indicate that they were treated in hospital, and then 'disposed of' by ship to unspecified destinations.

In the gentler surroundings of the churchyard on the hill, the bones of Hanibal Richards lie undisturbed. Whatever we think about the chances of life after death, it seems we share a near-universal desire for the mortal remains of the dead to stay where they are put. In some parts of medieval England, that desire – or the fear which stokes it – was so strong that it was customary to break up the corpse with an axe to prevent it from leaving its resting place, wandering into the village and seeking redress from the living. No need for such extreme measures here; old Hanibal Richards has been dead for over a hundred years, and whatever he was like in life, he has since death stayed securely lodged underground and caused no trouble to anyone.

The memory of him is written not only on this sober headstone but also into the buildings and even the topography. When I lived here, one of my favourite swimming places was a tiny, secluded beach under high cliffs, accessible by clambering over the rocks from Lee at low tide, or by taking the path over the headland and down a precipitous wooden staircase bolted to the cliff-face. On the map this beach bears the bland and barely appropriate name of Sandy Cove; in truth the sand is grey and gritty, but there are narrow inlets between the rocks, and on a calm day you can swim around from one to the next, hauling out like a seal every now and then to rest.

Cut into the cliff above the beach is a small cave which served as Hanibal's lookout. Below, where I have often stood wrapped in a towel after a swim, his pilots waited to guide illicit boats into the cove. The contraband would be unloaded and carried up the cliff path to waiting donkey carts, which conveyed it to various hiding places in the village.

On a tranquil afternoon, when nothing disturbs the calm water but a couple of sea kayaks, you can think you have the character of that place mapped out and understood. It functions as a retreat, a place to get away from the bad stuff. The narrow winding lanes put distance between you and the office, the traffic, the rolling news updates. But for the traveller on foot or on horseback those lanes were steep and arduous, and the terrain between Ilfracombe and Morte Point was wild country: inaccessible, insecure, and hard to police. The simple realities of geography made Lee a place which could live by its own rules and get away with it.

In his secluded cave, Hanibal was well hidden from the authorities, out of sight of the new coastguard cottage perched high on the cliff above the village. The problems of smuggling and piracy had intensified since his arrival, and the excise cutters which patrolled the coast were unable to control them. The decision to station a coastguard there signalled a concerted effort to crack down, but it was not easy on that ragged shoreline with its reefs and passages and lurking places.

He left traces in the village too. The old chapel of St Wardrede has been converted into a holiday cottage, complete with gas barbecue and tennis court. But in Hanibal's day it was derelict, used as a cowshed, and doubled as a lock-up where smuggled goods could be stashed. One report logs the contents of a cache discovered there by the customs men: 66 bottles of gin, 13 gallons of Portuguese red wine, 250 pounds of salt, and a box containing 73 packs of playing cards, each one missing the Ace of Spades.

Events at Rapparee Cove had made a hole in my understanding of this town. I needed to go back and see the place again, and think about what it all meant. I made contact with Pat, and he agreed to be my guide. We walked round the harbour-side, past the pink and blue washed fishermen's cottages, the shack where fresh fish is sold, the dinghies and canoes propped on end against the wall, the stacked lobster pots. We took the path leading up onto the cliff, past a skate park where four boys were practising, wordless and intense. The day was calm, the boats at anchor were still, the only sea-sound the low ticking of their masts.

I had not been here for many years, and the way was not as I remembered it. A memorial stone had been installed on the steps down to the cove, but there were no signs to guide visitors there. On a map beside the path, it seemed to be marked in the wrong place. I followed Pat down the steps to the beach, which was cut in two by a diagonal wedge of shadow. He was talking about the word 'slave', and how it had divided the town: there were those who welcomed the chance to re-examine the past, and those who wanted him to shut up and go away. Ilfracombe was not ready for this, he said. The town filled up with reporters on the trail of a sensational story. Official visitors from St Lucia were chauffeured in to see the site and talk to him about his research. A spectacular commemoration was held right here on the beach, attended by an African tribal chief, spiritualists, drummers and a choir. Meanwhile, he was lectured and threatened – on the phone, on the radio, by letter – by people who declared that it was all nonsense. The bones were of local people. Or they were from other shipwrecks entirely. He had got it all wrong. They knew for sure that *there were no slaves on board the* London.

'Obsessed' was Pat's own word. As he talked that day, he struck me as someone who had never lost the intense curiosity of childhood. There was a streak of naivety or stubbornness in him which made him willing to keep following a lead, regardless of scorn or censure. Rapparee Cove was one in a small constellation of subjects which had gripped him all his life: among others he mentioned antique bottles, medieval armour, and the north Devon rock-and-roll scene. He was an enthusiast by nature, painstaking in his inquiries, a collector of objects but also of knowledge. His research into the *London* was something he did for its own sake, never expecting it to draw much attention. It must have been like a bomb going off in his life.

He led me to the site at the back of the beach, right under the cliff, where the earth had been loosened and scraped away by recent tides. Part of the retaining wall was still standing, and there were almost certainly more human remains concealed behind it. Others were buried deep in the sand beneath our feet. This was still a graveyard. That day the sea was in the gentlest of moods, the water as clear as I'd ever seen it, but in a storm – perhaps this coming winter, or maybe twenty years from now – there would be another shift, another collapse, another trove of bones exposed. We trudged over the sand, and Pat talked about the coins he had found here over the years: Portuguese *reais*, Johannas, a gold dobra. He stopped suddenly to pick something up and put it in my hand. It was not what I expected. Not a piece of eight, but a single yellow stone.

We called in for a drink at the Britannia Arms on the harbour, where nothing much had changed since my last visit. But as I settled at a table near the fireplace, that easy sense of familiarity was broken. Pat gestured to something which my eyes must surely have rested on before without actually seeing. Hanging from a huge nail on the mantelpiece, between a battered horseshoe and a pair of fire tongs, was an old 'dead-eye', an iron ring with three holes used to guide the line of rigging on a sailing vessel. There was a faded label attached with string, which read 'HMS *London*. Raperee. Slave ship all hands lost'.

I'm looking at these two burial places, and seeing how differently time has treated them. The one where I'm standing now is on high ground, safe from storms and tides. It has been washed and mellowed by rain and sun, becoming a lush, official wilderness where I have ambled pleasurably today, reading the stones and wondering what it means to find an old outlaw tucked in cosily among the respectable drowned of this place.

The other is much more the kind of place where I might have expected to find him: a rugged scrap of territory lying outside the civic bounds, pounded and scoured by the sea. Instead it takes in the corpses, some still in chains, from a mass drowning 4,000 miles from home. And within a generation or two everyone has forgotten, and the graveyard becomes a pleasure beach.

When I stood and gazed across the harbour all those years ago, I was looking through the wrong end of the binoculars. Instead of magnifying, they made everything look smaller and less significant than it really was.

In the town museum, there is a watercolour of the wreck of the *London*. The ship languishes on the rocks. A man is visible in the sea, gesturing ambiguously: he might seem to be enjoying a swim, but he's probably stretching out his arms in the direction of the lifeboat which has put out from the harbour towards it. Three more large ships roll on a heavy sea; they are huge, dwarfing Capstone Hill and St Nicholas's Chapel as if they were toys. The drama moves out from the storm like ripples from a tossed stone, each ring weaker than the one before. On clifftop vantage points, groups of people stand and watch. In the foreground, cattle graze and a trio of lambs frisk unseasonably, oblivious to the catastrophe unfolding behind them.

The Annual Register for the year 1796 contains this entry:

This evening a very melancholy accident occurred at Ilfracombe. A ship, called the *London*, from St Kitts, having on board a considerable number of blacks (French prisoners) was driven on the rocks near to the entrance of the pier during a violent gale of wind, by which about 50 of the prisoners were drowned. Those who got on shore exhibited a most wretched spectacle, and the scene altogether was too shocking for description.

Even for a town accustomed to shipwreck and drowning, fifty was an appalling death toll. But there is another explosive dimension to the story of the *London*. According to one account, townspeople rushed to the scene of the shipwreck and did all they could to save the lives of those on board. Some rescuers are said to have shown great heroism, and three died in the attempt. But elsewhere it has been told very differently. When the wall collapsed and the bones fell out, an old argument fell out with them. How exactly did these men die?

It was not the first time this question had split opinion. 'It is well known by many old men now living,' wrote one of the two anonymous newspaper correspondents, back in 1856,

that sixty years ago a vessel manned by blacks, ran ashore, and that the then best families in town (being nothing but wreckers and smugglers) murdered the crew and buried the bodies on the beach, and then plundered the vessel of a very valuable cargo, consisting of ivory, doubloons, jewels, and etc. This having caused some disturbance, put an end to the system; otherwise, in bad weather, a common custom was to affix lanterns to horses tails, and lead them about the cliffs,

to decoy vessels. Many near descendants of the actual wreckers of the before-named vessel still reside here, and rank
amongst the most respectable of the inhabitants. The people
here still retain the name of 'combe sharks' which appellation
was bestowed upon them by the surrounding neighbourhood
about a century ago.

It was a scandalous claim, provoking outrage among the good
people of Ilfracombe. A second correspondent called the first 'a
wicked wretch', and accused him of slander. No evidence was produced to corroborate his story, but it certainly touched a nerve.

When the *London* went down, Hanibal Richards would have
heard about it by morning. It's only an hour's walk over the Torrs
to Lee, where he had now been resident for seven years, making his
living the way Coppinger had taught him, keeping the illicit boats
coming by night and the cowsheds and cellars stocked with contraband. There were others like him on this wild coast, living in plain
sight at the heart of their communities but staying beyond the reach
of the law. Did some of them also lure ships onto the rocks from
time to time? Were Hanibal and his gang, like the combe sharks,
prepared to wreck a ship and see a man drown? Or are the donkey
with the lantern tied to its tail and the young woman with the
pitchfork nothing more than lurid fictions?

The bones were taken away for testing, but the results were
inconclusive. The town may search its soul, but it's a very long time
ago and we will never be sure what happened at Rapparee Cove.
Accounts of the fatal night, written at different times and from different points of view, offer their own perspectives on the disaster and
its aftermath. Each is designed for a particular audience and crafted
for maximum effect. By the time they were written down, these tales
had already been told and retold many times: in the inn, at the fire-
side, from the pulpit, on the fishing boat. Like memories themselves,
stories are constructed anew on every telling, pulled together out of
their constituent parts into a slightly different shape each time.

In the sleepy graveyard, among the foxgloves where the bees drone and stagger, I sit in the sun and unfold a photocopy of one nineteenth-century account. In vivid terms, it tells how the *London* almost made it to shelter that night. It drew close to the pier, just yards from safe harbour, but the storm was so violent that it couldn't be secured. It lurched away again, and was dragged inexorably towards the Rapparee rocks. A young pilot called John Phillips Chiswell rowed out bravely in the storm to offer assistance, but the captain, seeing all too well that the ship was doomed, and knowing that the hold was loaded with human freight, would not allow him to board.

'Where are you from?' yelled Chiswell over the sound of the wind and waves.

'From Hell,' screamed back the captain, 'and bound for Damnation!'

A Wing and a Prayer

Who has been decapitating the angels? The police don't have much to go on, but there is some CCTV evidence suggesting that the culprit is a lone male. There is no obvious motive, and these cannot be opportunistic crimes. To climb the locked gates of a cemetery at night, carrying a substantial weapon – axe, sword, crossbow? – must take planning and dedication. And we are not talking about an isolated incident, but a co-ordinated series of attacks. One newspaper is calling it a *rampage*.

My local graveyard has not been targeted, but nevertheless most of the angels are missing something: if not the head, an arm or two. The more elaborate the gesture, the higher the likelihood of damage. One has been reduced to a draped torso, as pitiful as a fly in the playground with its wings torn off. Her neighbour stares, wide-eyed with incomprehension, at the empty space above her head where her own upraised arm used to be, like an amputee sensing a phantom limb.

Aside from these mutilations, this whole host conforms to a limited set of conventions about what an angel looks like: wings, curly hair and flowing robe. All are nubile young women, and their demure expressions are juxtaposed with sensuous curves and revealing drapery. It's an aesthetic based less on biblical foundation than on a late Victorian ideal of femininity. Many pose with downcast eyes, holding a sheaf of gathered corn or a wreath. Others clasp their hands in prayer, and one raises her fist in cryptic salute.

In the Christian tradition, angels are agents of God, commissioned to carry out special tasks: to take messages, to execute justice, to act as intermediaries and guardians, sometimes of individuals and sometimes of entire tribes or nations. They are essentially spirit, but they appear in physical form when there is momentous news to impart – pregnancy, birth, return from the dead. The message is not always unequivocally welcome, and the apparition can be terrifying. An angel is not like a person – it has no human character – but neither is it godlike. It is *other*.

The graveyard angel is a tamer manifestation. Her mission is to act as a link between this world and the next, between the mourner standing disconsolately under the dripping trees and the continuing life of the departed loved one, which is taking place out of sight and beyond reach. Sometimes she is seen watching over the deceased, and sometimes escorting the soul to heaven. The tranquillity in her face provides a counterweight to the pain and chaos of human grief, a suggestion that there is another realm in which this loss is not the crippling disaster it feels like, here and now, to parent or spouse or friend. Her smooth beauty is cast in hard and enduring stone, implying that though age and death afflict us in our mortal lives we will rise above them when we die. She prays for the soul of the departed, intercedes on his behalf, facilitates acceptance into heaven and accompanies him on the journey into the unknown.

Religious observance may have fallen away, but angels are far from obsolete: a third of Britons profess to believe in them. Yet even in the relative free-for-all of the modern cemetery, the range is surprisingly limited. Each angel holds a dove or a heart, or folds her hands in prayer. But nowadays beautiful young females are greatly outnumbered by cherubs: winged infants in sentimental poses, kneeling precociously in prayer or sleeping on curled feathers or open books.

Here, in the old graveyard, the vocabulary is more traditional: the sheaf is the life brought to harvest, the trumpet a call to resurrection on the Day of Judgement. Nineteenth-century masons worked from pattern books, and popular designs were repeated again and again. The turn of the century saw the beginnings of mass production, with customers choosing monuments off the peg. For years the fashion was for draped urns, then suddenly everyone wanted an angel.

Elsewhere in the world, the serenity of the angel may be tested and even broken. The Cimitero Acattolico in Rome has its famous Angel of Grief, collapsed and weeping over the tomb, condemned to an eternity of mourning without consolation. It's a figure imitated many times in American cemeteries, but it never caught on in England.

Perhaps it seemed to go against the natural order. After all, if the angel itself is felled by grief, what help is there for mere mortals? Who will guard, escort and intercede for us? Who will keep the offices of heaven? And if even the angels cannot keep their distance from human emotion and hold our individual losses in proportion, won't we frail creatures be engulfed and destroyed by it?

IV

The graveyard at dusk. See how the clamour of
things is countered always by the wish to disappear. Not to cease existence, but to let go the
strain of being distinct: the *this* and *this* of
it, the tyranny of attention. Dusk understands,
does what it can. Everything is rinsed by shadow;
yew and stone slip off the old integrities.

Miasma

When a graveyard is pictured in a book, or a scene in a film or play, it is generally attended by fog. It's a trope, a set piece of pathetic fallacy, a swirl of instant atmosphere. Fog locates the audience in the right psychic space, and delivers a reassuring shiver down the spine. Whatever this place means to us, the fog makes explicit. We are in the midst of mystery and ambiguity, and the fog is a kind of haunting. As well as making things murky and sinister, it chills the bones of the living, reminding them of the cold and wet undoing the dead beneath their feet. It's there in the vocabulary, when we talk about a 'pall' of mist, or of fog 'shrouding' the landscape. *Dust to dust,* says the Book of Common Prayer, although on a typical day in an English graveyard the prevailing element is mud.

The countryside is foggier than the city, because buildings and roads are much slower than trees and plants to lose their heat. However, London – built in a river basin, and sheltered by hills to the north – has had its own special relationship with fog, and the city churchyard, swathed in yellowish smog, is also a recurring image. Here it holds an old association of unwholesomeness. Smog is rich in pollution, but there's something else suspended in or between those water droplets. As the fog is pumped from a machine in the wings and drifts across the stage, it stirs an old memory, a collective fear of mortal disease.

Before the late nineteenth century and the arrival of germ the-ory, the prevailing explanation for the spread of contagious diseases was that they were carried in vapours, or 'miasma', emanating from decaying organic matter. Bad air could make you sick, not only for the reasons we would think of today – coal smoke, the fumes of industry – but because it contained the infectious agents of cholera and typhoid and all the other catastrophic illnesses that swept through families and neighbourhoods with such terrifying speed. No bad air could be worse than that coming from the corpses of those who had died of such diseases, and the graveyard was a place of mortal danger. A surgeon called George Walker, known as 'Graveyard Walker', published an influential book on the subject: *Gatherings from Grave Yards; Particularly Those of London: with a Concise History of the Modes of Interment Among Different Nations, from the Earliest Periods. And a Detail of Dangerous and Fatal Results Produced by the Unwise and Revolting Custom of Inhuming the Dead in the Midst of the Living*. The book is a compilation of Walker's own research, the findings of other medical scientists, and ghastly anecdotes illustrating the risks. A gravedigger disturbs a previous burial and dies an agonising death himself. A mass grave is left uncovered for four weeks, and a local epidemic follows. A vault is reopened and churchgoers fall ill en masse. Walker's campaign was intended to horrify and outrage its readers, and to bring about changes in burial practices, particularly in urban churchyards, which at that time were without exception overcrowded and badly managed. He was particularly damning about the ways in which this affected the poor, whose cramped dwellings were squeezed in close to the churchyard, who breathed its odours, drew their drinking supplies from its groundwater, and were daily subjected to the sight of smashed coffins and rotting corpses. His mission was the improvement of public health and living conditions, and his book was meant to be a call to action. Some of the gruesome incidents described in its pages are no less shocking today.

But Walker was wrong about miasma. The science changed, and with it our understanding of the vectors of infectious disease. The stench of the churchyard must indeed have been enough to turn the stomach, but it did not spread typhus. However, there is still a lingering suspicion about the graveyard and its vapours. The image of fog seeping between gravestones acts as a visual reminder of old fears: a sign of pestilence, a warning. When I was a child, I would hold my breath as I passed the village churchyard, which according to my friend Alison was a tried-and-tested method of avoiding ending up there myself. Perhaps this was not pure superstition, but a last remnant of what had once been considered a sensible health precaution.

Anxiety about miasma shaded into necrophobia. At times Walker's language turns accusatory. 'A diluted poison is given in exchange from the dead to the living,' he declares. Infection as a kind of malicious gift from the deceased – revenge, perhaps, on those who have survived them. He writes too of 'the pestiferous exhalations of the dead', as if, heedless of the extinction of life, they continued somehow to exercise its vital functions: puffing out their plaguey breath as an act of spite against those who hurried them underground and turned back to their pleasures and comforts as if nothing had changed.

In truth, graveyards are no more prone to fog than anywhere else. It's a simple consequence of the ground cooling and a layer of air then cooling by contact with it; when dew point and air temperature are equal, the moisture condenses into millions of tiny droplets which break and scatter the light. It's just weather. But like all weather, it transforms place. It confuses our senses, distorting perception of speed and distance. Visibility is reduced, with everything rendered in lower contrast like a poor photocopy or a set of slides in a brightly lit lecture theatre. The water droplets attenuate sound, sometimes creating a muffling effect, sometimes sharpening and clarifying the acoustics so that we jump when someone coughs a hundred yards away.

A light fog in a graveyard can look gauzy and benign. It softens colours and blurs lines, reminding us that death and life are not cut off from one another but invariably exist together, in the same space. It can for a moment help to assuage our griefs and terrors, smoothing the picture. To introduce swirling mist into the scene is to apply the usual filter, and to make us experience a familiar set of feelings. The dead are veiled, but close. Death itself loses its distinction, becomes nebulous, equivocal.

Crank up the machine and pump out a thick fog and things get claustrophobic. Now it seems to wall us in, separating us from everyday life and all that is benign and predictable. It traps us within a space in which the usual rules do not apply. It rubs out familiar landmarks, making navigation experimental and fraught with hazard. The ground is obscured from view, and the audience is on the edge of its seat, waiting for something to break through, like a skeletal hand shoved up from a grave. As we grope our way forward, objects loom up without warning. It's impossible to scan the surroundings. Are we alone, or is someone – or something – prowling stealthily behind? Disorientated, we start to fear we are truly lost, cast out into a wasteland beyond the lights and voices of the village. We fear we will stumble about forever in a featureless space without definition, without edges. We fear the extinction of meaning. Nothingness.

Fog like this has the quality of a bad dream. It tends to form at night, and clear soon after dawn, when the air temperature rises and the water droplets evaporate. When the morning sun burns it off, the brightness and logic of the day replaces it. This is the essence of our double life: the rational everyday self, strolling calmly between the graves, pausing to read an inscription as if reading a text message; and the primal self, still governed by the reptilian brainstem with its prehistoric fears and intuitions. And so, here on the page, the stage or the screen, the weather is closing in and the age-old scene is set once more. I shiver from the damp air, the cold earth underfoot, the prickling scalp. This is the theatre of the graveyard, with its smoke and mirrors: the dry ice of the fog, and the headstone where I see myself dimly reflected: *As you are now, so once was I.*

Oh Lovely Child

'The fact that the misfortune of poverty could qualify a person for dismemberment after death became too intensely painful for contemplation; became taboo. The memory went underground of a fate literally unspeakable.'

Ruth Richardson, *Death, Dissection, and the Destitute*

St Ebbe's does not have a churchyard, but a garden: a square of patchy grass and snowdrops where the churchyard used to be. There's a bench under a tree, and a robin scuffling for grubs in a heap of dead leaves.

Thirty years have passed since I lived in Oxford. Now I have slipped through the side gate into the garden, and it's as if I'd never really been away. I have taken my habitual place on the same old bench where I would often sit. Back then I had a temporary job in a department store on Queen Street, and this was a good place to get away from the crowd and eat my lunch in peace. I would throw on a coat over my scratchy polyester uniform and escape from the hushed and soporific shop floor, eager to *feel* something, even if it was only the noise of the traffic and the metallic cold on my face. There would always be tourists queueing at the foot of Carfax Tower, waiting their turn to climb the ninety-nine steps and photograph the dreaming spires. I would turn in the opposite direction and branch off down a narrow side street towards the river. There the blankly familiar shopfronts gave way to red-brick and mock-Tudor facades, and the glass entrance of Westgate shopping centre pressed close to the old church, where I would slip through the gate from the street into the garden. There was rarely anyone else here, though the signboard declared that we were welcome.

It's Sunday morning, and yet that same route was livelier than ever today. As I turned down the side street, I walked into an enormous flock of helium balloons tethered to the pavement, jostling and rustling in the breeze. I was lost for a moment in a swarm of dolphins and unicorns, cartoon characters and oversized champagne bottles. I fought my way through, and arrived at Penny Farthing Place, where the many bicycles of the faithful were chained to the railings. As I passed the open door of the church I saw it was packed with young people waiting for the service to begin. Now, from my seat outside, I hear first a burst of laughter, then brief but thunderous applause, followed by the more predictable sound of a hymn starting up.

There is an evangelical tradition here which has its roots in a crisis that gripped the church nearly 200 years ago, when the rector was declared incurably insane. Despite committal to a lunatic asylum, he could not for contractual reasons be removed from his post, and the consequence was that for the fifty remaining years of his life his duties were covered by a series of idealistic young curates. What they lacked in experience was more than compensated for by energy and a sense of mission. They founded schools, fed the destitute and visited the sick and dying; several succumbed themselves after contracting cholera or smallpox in the course of this work. On the strength of their commitment to community work they built up the affection and trust of their parishioners, and during those 50 years the congregation doubled, then tripled, so that at its height more than 600 people squeezed into this church on Sundays.

All that cholera filled up the churchyard. In 1843 the council ordered that burials should cease here and in all of Oxford's churchyards, and at the workhouse and the gaol. Land was purchased for municipal cemeteries, and burial of the dead moved away from parish churches and out from the city centre to the urban fringe.

More recently, most of the signs of death have been cleared from this place, in order to make room for the practical needs of the living. This now serves as an outdoor space for play-schemes and toddler groups, and as somewhere for churchgoers to stand and chat over coffee after morning service. Weak sunshine pools on the early crocuses, and among them several squashed and unpeeling tennis balls; it's a place for recreation rather than mourning. Most of the gravestones have gone, and the few that remain stand stiffly against the railings, looking on at all this frivolity like a row of old aunts at a disco. Many are heavily eroded, blackened by weather. But when I walk between them this morning I pause to examine one whose inscription is still partly legible:

> OH LOVELY CHILD, IN HOPE FOR HEAV'N DESIGNED
> NOT LEFT TO KNOW THE TROUBLES OF MANKIND.
> THO HUMAN FRAILTIES MAKE THY PARENTS WEEP
> YET —— CHILD ENTOM'D DOST SWEETLY SLEEP.
>
> EARTHLY PARADISE IS SOFTLY FLED
> —— TILL CHRIST SHALL RAISE THE DEAD.
> —————— THE SOUL TRANSLATE
> ————————————— SO GREAT.

I recognise the verse. I've seen it before – or at least something very like it. It's a variant of a popular Victorian epitaph, received, reconfigured a little, recycled. A chunk of pure sentiment, not unlike the verses which appear in the obituary columns of local papers today. Stooping to read it again, trying to fill in the gaps where the words have worn away, I find myself thinking of two young children called Richard and Amelia. They have been waiting at the edge of my thoughts all morning. They were buried here in 1893, fifty years after the official notice to close the churchyard. This is not their grave, but they come to mind nonetheless.

Hackneyed, yes. Pious, certainly. But that opening line still catches at the heart. The stone tells me nothing about the particular child it commemorates – no name, age, cause of death. But it says something about the parents, and about *all* parents. The pain of this loss was cancelled neither by hopes of heaven nor by rain and soot. *Oh lovely child.*

After a few months spent pricing and folding stock, and handing out plastic numbers at the fitting rooms, I went to college and trained to be a teacher. I lived with my boyfriend in a rented flat, which occupied the ground floor of a tiny terraced house in Headington. That was the dampest habitation I have known: clothes stored in the wardrobe grew spotted with mould, and slugs trailed across the kitchen lino and up the walls. The rooms were stacked in a row front to back, and when we had friends to stay they slept on the lumpy old settee and tiptoed apologetically past the foot of our bed to get to the bathroom. We owned a tiny black-and-white television on which everything was seen through a continuous blizzard of interference. We had access to a thin strip of wild garden, where the grass had not been cut for years and next door's roses tumbled in perfumed anarchy over the rickety fence. We kept our bicycles under an elder bush near the back door, and in summer the saddles and handlebars were sticky all over with honeydew.

We were lucky to land a place in Headington. There were shops and pubs and an independent cinema. There was a grand old house converted to a public library, and a park where the local kids spent Sunday afternoons rolling on the lawns and scrambling down the ha-ha. There was an ancient path called Cuckoo Lane, overhung with beech trees and may blossom, that led all the way into town. To the north, our road meandered off into the past: the honey-coloured Cotswold stone village of Old Headington. Its parish church had a Norman arch, and an ornate brass lamp which had burned perpetually on the altar since 1142. In its peaceful churchyard, some of the stones were so deeply submerged that only the top few inches were visible, just a scrolled strip and a carved skull catching the sun here and there. In the shade of a huge yew tree, there was a riddle of an epitaph:

HERE LYETH JOHN

WHO TO YE KING DID BELONG

HE LIVD TO BE OLD

AND YET DYED YOUNG

The footstone delivered the punchline:

IN MEMORY OF JOHN YOUNG

WHO DIED NOV 9 1688

AGED 100 YEARS

They are only three miles apart, but Headington and St Ebbe's belong to two separate Oxfords. The locals used to say you only had to breathe to know it: down here in the city the air was like stale beer, and up there on the hill it was pure champagne.

Time had dealt the two places very different hands. While Headington hung on to its village inns and cottage gardens, St Ebbe's was utterly transformed. The slums were cleared, the narrow streets demolished, the land was stripped, levelled and concreted over. Where once the zealous curates ducked in and out of those overcrowded houses on their ministry to the poor and the sick, there was now a shopping centre, all brick tower and plate glass, and a multi-storey car park. The church survived, and its graveyard was repurposed as a garden. By then it had been officially closed to burials for 140 years.

Exceptions were made, however. In the decades after the official order to cease was issued, the ground was occasionally opened and a burial performed, discreetly and with the minimum of ceremony, and without any stone to mark the place. It was like that with Richard, and then with Amelia. There was no funeral cortege, no family gathered at the graveside. A basic ritual was followed, and the modest cost was borne by the university's Anatomy School, which had purchased their bodies from Radcliffe Infirmary and dissected them. Like thousands more, they had become commodities in a lively trade supplying corpses for medical research.

This was not the illicit trade of the 'resurrection men' who resorted to grave-robbing and murder to meet demand. These were regular transactions, sanctioned by the state and organised to happen as discreetly as possible, out of sight at the back doors of hospitals and workhouses in towns all over England. Improvements in the treatment of disease required medical research, and medical research required corpses. The logical place to source them was in the poorest part of town, because anyone who could afford it chose the things money could buy: a coffin, a space in the family plot, a headstone with a loving inscription, flowers for the grave. So powerfully did people want these things that they would pawn or sell their possessions to pay for them, or would borrow the money at exorbitant rates of interest. Where friends and neighbours were in a position to contribute, they would have a whip-round. Anything to secure a decent funeral. And so it was invariably the poorest of the poor – those with nothing to pawn, and no one to help – who ended up on the dissection table.

Richard and Amelia were among the poorest of the poor. They and their families lived in an area developed for housing in the construction boom of the 1820s and '30s, when speculators were scrambling to buy up land and meet the demand created by a rapidly expanding urban population. But it was too close to the river and too low-lying to be suitable for quality housing. St Ebbe's depended for drainage on open ditches and watercourses, and the narrow, badly paved streets and tiny urban cottages which were crammed in here suffered right from the start from flooding, leading directly to a series of cholera outbreaks. A survey noted 'a degree of neglect and filth rarely witnessed' and described the new development as 'a swamp converted into a cesspool'. An early photograph is carefully framed to provide a selective view: it shows the river meandering contentedly around a patch of water-meadow where cattle graze, and the sun breaking through clouds to illuminate the famous skyline of spires and domes. Over it all streams a banner of smoke from the gasworks chimney. But the railway bridge built over the river to carry coal to the works is out of shot, and so are the cramped streets where the workers lived, died and gave up their bodies to the anatomists.

I knew nothing about any of this when I took a break from the long day of shop work and came to sit here on this bench in the church garden, with my tuna sandwich and my copy of *Deschooling Society*. This place only came to mean something to me the following year, when I spent a brief but unforgettable few weeks on Blackbird Leys, the estate built to rehouse the people of St Ebbe's when their neighbourhood was demolished. During that summer, which I remember with blinding intensity thirty years later, I learned a little about loss, displacement, the way a community survives and changes when it is uprooted.

It was during that summer that I first heard about this grim bit of history: bodies traded for dissection, and the knife falling on poor parts of the city where people could not escape it. I learned that this piece of the past was a secret, a source of shame and sorrow nearly a century on. These were events so traumatic that they had left few visible traces and were almost impossible to talk about. So I went back again to St Ebbe's, to this churchyard, to the plot of ground which knew that history well, which still held the cell and fibre of it. I walked back and forth over its tussocky grass, as if trying to read it through the soles of my feet and up through my body. As if by wanting hard enough I could understand everything that had happened there. I was twenty-three, still young enough to half believe in such a thing.

The slum clearance began in the 1950s, and the area changed forever. The entire population was removed and decanted into the new estate, beyond the city fringes – or as one of the early residents put it, the arse-end of nowhere. While St Ebbe's was being razed to the ground, Blackbird Leys underwent its own dramatic reinvention: from sewage farm to new town. Before construction began, the only residents were the occupants of a row of old farm cottages, one of whom recalls playing among the raised vegetable beds fertilised by sewage: 'As youngsters we would search for the nests and eggs of the lapwing or peewit, leaping from quaking bog to quaking bog, often as not getting a shoeful of the vile muck as a reward for our pains.' He and his neighbours were incredulous when they heard the plans to build hundreds of new houses there.

Within a few years, St Ebbe's was wiped off the face of the earth. The construction of the Westgate centre obliterated the old streets, and another round of redevelopment has since deleted the first. But until recently it was possible to see, between windswept expanses of tarmac, fragments of kerb from the old road alignments. I tried to copy them into a sketchbook, feeling in some obscure way they mattered. The wind keened around the concrete battlements of the shopping centre. When it was opened, there was a futuristic moving walkway; it was envisaged that customers would step from their cars and ride to the shops without having to brave the weather. But it broke down almost immediately, and by the time I came to live here it was standing derelict, littered with smashed bottles and dead pigeons.

Back in the sparkling air of Headington, the slugs crept over a poster on our kitchen wall depicting Norman Tebbit with his leg cocked over a bicycle. Planes took off from an airbase a few miles away and dropped bombs on Libya. There was an incident at a power station in Russia, and I peered through the blizzard of interference to watch the news: scientists holding Geiger counters over the wet grass in Cumbria, against a background of sheep grazing obliviously in the sunshine. I tried to concentrate on preparing for the long teaching practice that would make the difference between qualifying or not. I learned that my placement was to be not in the golden triangle of Summertown, Kidlington and Witney, with the precocious sons and daughters of dons, but on the Blackbird Leys estate. I regarded this as good news. I was interested in Oxford's split personality: the tensions between town and gown, between the dreaming spires and the other districts where the living was not so easy. This would be a chance to see one of the other Oxfords from the inside. I knew very little about Blackbird Leys, but I was aware that it was going through hard times. Its main source of employment, the motorworks at Cowley, had gone into decline, and unemployment was running high. The *Oxford Mail* ran reports of twocking and joyriding and knife crime. It may have started out in a spirit of optimism – new homes for everyone, with proper bathrooms and gas fires – but by the time I turned up with my rucksack full of radical educational theory, Blackbird Leys was notorious.

Each morning I would tug my bike out of the elder bush, wipe off the rain and honeydew, and pedal away down Windmill Road with its suburban front doors and garden paths, resisting the temptation to divert to the intriguing churchyard at Headington Quarry where William 'Merry' Kimber, Father of the English Morris, is buried under a stone carved in the shape of a concertina and bell-pads. I took the cycle track by the ring road, and when the two tower blocks rose into view – Windrush first, then Evenlode – I had crossed a threshold from one Oxford to another. No ha-has or morris-dancing here. This was a place with a reputation. My tutor had summoned me and spoken tactfully about it. Had I perhaps read that the estate was a dangerous hinterland of disaffection and delinquency? Typical media stereotyping and smear. True, it scored highly on all the usual indicators of social deprivation. Yes, there were Challenges. But he would like me to go there with an open mind, and to remember what John Holt said in *How Children Fail*: 'There is no way to coerce children without making them afraid'. As I stood to leave, he warned me not to carry any valuables with me, and recommended I stay on school premises over the lunch break.

If I close my eyes, I can summon up a brief memory of arriving for the first time at the school, wheeling my bike through the entrance gate and wondering where I should be going. Everything is grey: school buildings, playground, sky. I'm absurdly early. I try to push the recollection further, to see what happens next – my hand on the gate, the first few children arriving – but the memory disperses like a curl of cigarette smoke. I do remember that it was a wonderful school. The buildings were ugly and dilapidated, but the teachers were the warmest and most dedicated I've met before or since. The teacher supervising me was a brilliant, funny, motherly woman who treated each one of her hungry, hyperactive charges with the same respect, affection and serious encouragement as if they'd been star pupils at Radley a few miles downriver. It was that teacher who told me about the St Ebbe's connection, and the trade in bodies for medical research. They were kids like these, she said, gesturing around us. She had friends on the estate, but she would never raise this subject with them. It might seem like history to me, but something as harrowing as this could haunt families for generations. She broke off. She had noticed me surreptitiously checking the soles of my shoes, guessing the stench was something I'd trodden in from the pavement. No, she said in an undertone, it's Antony. Then she handed me a book. Why don't you sit down with Antony and hear him read?

I wonder what happened to Antony, that quiet loner who ate leftover crusts from the bin at lunchtime and fell asleep with his head on the desk most afternoons. I had so much to unlearn. My fancy theories were no use at all. What mattered was to sit close to the child who never washed. The challenge was to keep them in the building. It was a case of *How Teachers Fail*. On my second day, a boy kicked over a desk and ran out of my immaculately planned lesson, escaped from the school, stole a motorbike and crashed it into a shop window. I was distraught. I remember the head of maths and his deputy trying to cheer me up in the staff-room with a rendition of 'You Always Hurt the One You Love', with improvised percussion using teaspoons and pool cues.

*

Richard and Amelia were just two of many, but at least I now had their names. Without knowing exactly why, I went looking for them.

The parish registers had been carefully transcribed, the pages neatly typed and clipped into plastic ring-binders. Here I found the basic facts. I learned that they were buried two and a half months apart; the grave was dug for one and reopened for the next.

When I'd read the entries and copied them down in my note-book, I collected my things from the locker and went out into the street. But after a few paces I turned and retraced my steps back into the archives. It seemed impossible to leave it there. Those two children could not be reduced to nothing but their corpses. At least I had to know how they died. I went to the desk and filled in the slip and waited for the registers of Radcliffe Infirmary to be brought up from the storeroom. It seemed to take forever for the squeaking metal trolley to arrive with its load of books and maps and papers, and I noticed as I waited that my hands were clenched.

The registers were great leather-bound volumes, heavy, fragile at the spine. The pages were discoloured and thick to turn, the entries inked in several different hands. There were blots and cor-rections, places where the ink had been changed and the colour did not quite match. Those volumes were more than the information they contained.

Date of Admission: Sep. 18 1893.

Age: 5 weeks.

Trade, Calling, Service, or Condition of Life: None.

Nature of Disease or Lesion: General name on admission –
    Diarrhoea. Special name on discharge – Same.

When Discharged: Died, Sep. 20.

This was Richard, who died of 'summer complaint', a form of gas-troenteritis which afflicted the infants of poor families, a consequence of hand-feeding with a paste or 'pap' of bread and water, mixed with milk if any was available. In warm weather, pap was a breeding ground for bacteria, and the baby fed like this would be poorly nourished and weak, unable to fight off the infection.

Date of Admission: Nov. 9 1893.

Age: 4.

Trade, Calling, Service, or Condition of Life: None.

Nature of Disease or Lesion: General name on admission – Bronchio-pneumonia. Special name on discharge – Diphtheria with Ulcerated Throat.

When Discharged: Died, Dec. 3.

Here was Amelia, one of 6,404 people in England to die from diphtheria in 1893. Two-thirds of them were children.

Almost nothing has endured. Each of their lives was as brief as a flame lit in a draughty room and then blown out. Sitting at that table with that musty old slab of a book, it occurred to me that I might be the only person living who knew where they were born, and the names of their parents, and how they died, and what happened to them afterwards. It felt like a responsibility. I committed the details to memory – easy enough, they were so few. I must carry them like something infinitely precious which if spilt would never be gathered up again.

Beyond St Andrew's church, the village of Headington frays rustically into country lanes with cow-parsley and farm gateways. It looks as if you could set off with map and rucksack and have a day's walking in glorious, undisturbed countryside. But the pastoral margin is very narrow: the A40 slices through the fields a few hundred yards away, and the John Radcliffe Hospital sprawls over what was the manor house and its estate. These days the village is maintained as a kind of illusion, carefully preserved, complete with cottage gardens, old lamp-stands and black-on-white road signs. It is still possible to believe in it, if you stand in a certain place and look in the right direction and shut your ears to the roar of the modern world which is pressing in very close.

Appearances were kept up, too, at the graveside of Richard and Amelia. No stone to mark the place, but a cassocked priest checking his pocket-watch, a solemn voice reciting the usual words, *Forasmuch as it hath pleased Almighty God*, etc., the earth shovelled in quickly and the whole thing over without any fuss. Afterwards, there's no question of the family sharing their story with friends and neighbours; it's too painful and too shocking to talk about. At least the burial brings some privacy, at least it covers the raw wound. They had no choice. They have done what they could.

And at least they could be confident that the grave would not be disturbed. In their parents' day, body-snatching was a very real fear. There had always been money to be made from dead bodies, but back then it was a desperate and lawless business; unless a graveyard was guarded day and night it was impossible to be sure that the freshly interred would stay safely underground. Security had become less of a concern following the Anatomy Act of 1832, which provided the government with the power to confiscate the bodies of paupers who died in workhouses and hospitals, and to use them for the purposes of medical research.

Before the passing of the Anatomy Act, only convicted criminals were liable to forfeit their bodies after death; it was seen as part of the penalty paid for the offence. Extending the same treatment to the poor was received as a gross insult. 'I would recommend in the first place,' said Henry Hunt, MP for Preston,

that the bodies of all our Kings be dissected, instead of expending seven or eight hundred thousand pounds of the public money for their interment. Next, I would dissect all our hereditary legislators. After that, the bishops, with a host of those priests and vicars who feed themselves and not their flocks ... Were there a law passed to this effect, I would willingly consent that my body should be given 'for the promotion of science'.

Such arguments were written off as sentimental, melodramatic, and above all irrational. The law was passed and, a generation later, the trade in bodies really took off. New legislation created the demand; in a drive to raise professional standards, medical students were now required to pass a two-year course in Anatomy before they could qualify and practise as doctors. There was an acute shortage of corpses, until supply caught up in the 1880s and '90s, when a double-dip recession brought about a drastic change of approach by government towards the poor. A ruthless campaign was launched to cut welfare expenditure, with the intention of eradicating all 'outdoor relief' payments and forcing those who could not support themselves into the workhouse. One of the reliefs which was abolished was the burial payment, which had previously met the cost of a basic funeral: a coffin, a woollen shroud, an interment fee. Since the state would no longer help with these expenses, families without means were left with no choice but to forfeit the corpse.

The slums of St Ebbe's were a rich source of supply. This had always been an impoverished part of town, and the crusade against welfare deepened the misery still further. A lively body-trafficking market developed, all above board and within the law. Some politicians and public figures opposed it, but others approved, justifying it as the settling of a debt: the sale of a corpse brought in a pound or two, rather more if it was a young woman or an infant, and allowed government to recoup some of what it had spent on welfare payments during life. Poor relief was reimagined as a loan, mortgaged against the body. There was an inexorable logic to it all: it solved several problems at once. So the trade was regularised, and in true Victorian style an elaborate bureaucracy developed: detailed accounts, petty-cash books, special train carriages to carry the dead from one town to another, regulations about the labelling of body parts, minimum standards for burial (six to a grave, and a numbered wooden cross).

A photograph taken in 1893 shows the Dissecting Room of the Department of Human Anatomy, where the two children were taken from the Radcliffe Infirmary that same year. A dozen scrubbed wooden tables, lamps suspended on chains from the rafters. A statue, a skeleton.

In another photograph, the gentlemen of the Anatomy and Physiology class pose in their academic gowns and deadpan expressions, many of them holding exhibits: a human skull, a white rabbit, a giant egg, something which looks alarmingly like a mummified child. Anatomy was a gentleman's business; this was no place for women.

As my teacher-supervisor explained to me when I was twenty-three and knew nothing: poverty looks different from one generation to the next. Like a mutating virus, it adapts to the changing circumstances, exchanges its ragged trousers and bare feet for designer rip-off tracksuit and trainers. A child living in a house with a satellite dish may still be malnourished. It's a matter of going without – not just without food or clothes, but crucially without the power of choice. A decision was taken, St Ebbe's was torn down. Families were uprooted, communities divided and rehoused. Those who were personally affected had no say in the matter.

Antony, and the boy who stole the motorbike, and many of the kids I met that summer, were from old St Ebbe's families. Their great-grandparents would have played with Amelia in the street, and heard the news when Richard was born, or when he died. They were the descendants of those who were visited by the enthusiastic young chaplains when they were sick with cholera, or who lost their children first to diphtheria and then to the dissecting table. Those kids, now grown up with kids of their own, may be curious about the past, and where they fit in. But if they come back to visit the streets where their ancestors lived, or the graves where they were buried, they will find no trace of them here. And it occurs to me, as I sit in this tranquil garden with its brick path, bench and litter bin, that just as parents can lose their children, and lose them twice over, so a place can lose its people: both the living and the dead.

Blue

Despite the afternoon stillness, the curtain of ivy against the church-yard wall shakes out a few flakes of confetti. They are a lustrous blue, which makes me think of French window-shutters. Each flake rides uncertainly on an updraft for a moment, before finding its own direction. As it flies, its wings are sheeny and translucent in the late August sunlight, but when it rests on an ivy flower it folds its blue away as if to protect it from too much exposure, and the undersides are modest, like paper covers marked with a few spots of black ink.

It has been known by a sequence of descriptive names over the centuries: Azure Blue, Wood Blue, Blue-Speckt Butterfly. We know it now as the Holly Blue, but it might just as accurately be the Ivy Blue, since it is equally dependent on both plants. In a good year, there are two of these maiden flights: a spring brood emerging from the holly, and an autumn brood from the ivy. Both holly and ivy are ubiquitous churchyard plants, and the Holly Blue is a regular here, shimmering against their dark leaves and secretive flowers.

I have pored over the descriptions in my book of butterflies, in order to distinguish the Holly Blue from the Common Blue and the Small Blue, and to tell male from female. It's not easy, because they rarely stay still for long or display their open wings in a convenient position. Even at rest they quiver, part their wings halfway, and then squeeze them shut. There are subtle differences between the early and late broods, too, though of course they are never seen side by side except in pictures, where the wings of the autumn female are a darker shade of blue, their black borders drawn more thickly. The wing is shown in close-up, edged as if with a broader nib like a marker pen. I think suddenly of those black-edged funeral cards which were surely a Victorian custom, though I remember seeing one propped up behind the sweet tin on my grandparents' mantelpiece in the 1960s. It wasn't blue of course. These butterflies are gloriously blue, like chipped-off bits of sky. Even on a cold day they stake a claim for summer.

In the human imagination, butterflies are routinely enlisted to signify joy, hope, innocence and lightness of spirit. They have a special place in our affections, unlike so many of their fellow insects – crane-flies, bluebottles, even their close cousins, the moths. When it comes to our human appreciation of insects, there is a clear taxonomy: butterflies, bees and dragonflies are all more than acceptable, but the majority are greeted with varying degrees of squealing and swatting.

Perhaps we look at butterflies, as I'm looking now at these Holly Blues, and feel sure that something so beautiful must be pure and good. No matter that they spend a lot of their time on the ground, stalking over the mud and muck and sucking up salts and minerals. Their likenesses find their way onto stationery, jewellery, cake decorations. It's hard to imagine a sugar crane-fly on a birthday cake.

But all is not sweetness and light in the world of the Holly Blue, now flittering from one green flower to another. Like all butterflies, it goes through metamorphosis, a process which sounds to our ears like a kind of horror story, complete with flesh-dissolving enzymes and erupting genitals. But the Holly Blue also has a gruesome tendency to be eaten alive from the inside before it can complete the process.

The female lays her eggs in the holly or the ivy, depending on the season. She places them precisely, one at a time, at the base of a flower bud, to ensure a ready food supply later. After a fortnight or so, the egg hatches into a caterpillar. It's an insignificant pale-green colour, occasionally tinged with pink, but it's easy enough to find once you know what you're looking for: a flower bud with a hole punched in it, where the caterpillar has scooped out the nutritious centre. If you do spot one, it may well be attended by ants, which seem at a glance to be attacking it. In fact it's an irresistible kind of syrup the ants are after, secreted by glands on the caterpillar's body. Soon after hatching, it emits a chemical attractant which brings the ants hiking up the host plant to find it. So insatiable is their appetite for this honeydew that they will go to great lengths to protect their supply, guarding the caterpillar all day and dragging it into a more secluded position at night, tucked in under leaves or close to the branch where they can keep it out of sight of predators.

The arrangement suits the Holly Blue, maximising the chances of survival and successful metamorphosis into a butterfly. Some years it works like a charm, and the churchyard glitters with blue plenty, spring and autumn. Other years, however, the arrangement falls through. The chemical signal still goes out, the ants still climb into the holly or the ivy and track down the caterpillar. They carry out the same careful routines, guarding by day and concealing by night. But in these years, their attentions are not enough to protect the caterpillar against its nemesis, the parasitic wasp *Listrodomus nycthemerus*. For this species of wasp, the Holly Blue is the one host through which it can reproduce. The female wasp, perhaps alerted by the very same chemical signal, homes in on the caterpillar and injects it with a single egg. After hatching, the wasp larva grows, fattened on the flesh of its host: first caterpillar, then chrysalis. At the moment of truth, when the chrysalis breaks open, it's not a butterfly which emerges but a wasp.

When it comes to describing this extraordinary sequence of events, writers usually deploy a lexis of violence. The wasp is 'vicious' and 'remorseless', the Holly Blue its 'victim'. The laying of the egg and the development of the young wasp are characterised as acts of warfare, and the two species as locked together in mortal combat. But if we step back and view the situation over the longer term it looks more like a partnership: each population managing the other, the two achieving between them a state of equilibrium in which there are no winners or losers. The wasp is skilled and effective in finding the host it needs, and some years it is so successful that the Holly Blue population goes into a steep decline. Six or seven years will pass before the wasp, with no caterpillars left in which to lay its eggs, becomes so scarce itself that the Holly Blue picks up again, and people say what a good year it is for butterflies and it must be the early spring we had.

Churchyards have become important strongholds for the Holly Blue, and for a number of other species which depend on ivy. In gardens and parks, it's generally cut back before it can flower, but here there's a more laissez-faire approach to tidiness. A month from now the Holly Blues will be gone, but this curtain of ivy will be sumptuous with pale-green flower heads. By day it will be thrumming with bees. Walking at dusk, I'll breathe its primeval scent.

Everything else is just background: the people who come and go, the gravestones carefully marked with particular names. For the Holly Blue and the parasitic wasp, there's more at stake than individual survival. One generation, or even six, are not the point. There's a system at work, a repeating pattern in which each species plays its part. So elegantly do the two coexist and balance one another, the boundaries between them seem to dissolve and reveal them operating as a single entity. A bad year for one is a good year for the other. And although wasps are unlikely ever to rival butterflies in our human affections, they are equal in my eyes. *Listrodomus nycthemerus* is itself beautiful: a slender-waisted, glistening creature just half an inch long, aubergine-black streaked with citron, and wings like hammered silk. *Bugs Britannica* describes it as 'sinisterly handsome', but this is just more of the same old bias.

V

The graveyard in winter. On the tomb of Alexander Whitgift, a spider with five legs limps in a circle, stops and re-learns its losses. The goldcrest waits its moment in the yew.

Proof

Old gravestones are stacked in a corner behind the church, as if waiting to be taken to the tip. They have been uprooted to make way for an extension, allowing the church-hall facilities to be upgraded. With no one to claim them, they present a problem of disposal. But in other times, when the living was hard, stones like these would be pulled from the ground and carted away to floor houses and barns. The churchyard itself was a contested space, put to a variety of secular uses; from time to time it hosted village fairs, plays and even wrestling matches. Vestry minutes record complaints that memorial trees have been felled for timber, and that ploughing is encroaching on the graves. Dickens expressed his surprise on seeing an elderly couple in a city churchyard raking together 'an apronful of hay', but at time of want it was simply obvious that these resources, however paltry, should be harvested and used rather than going to waste.

I wish I could flick through the stack of old stones like books on a shelf. I wish I had a barn to floor, where I could kneel and read them. Each bears the trace of a human story, still just about tangible though the text is worn and defaced. You who departed this life in 1832, who were you? I see you were *faithful even unto death*, but your name is gone. Still, the very existence of the carved stone, timeworn and no longer marking the place, confers some fading material proof. It implies that your life amounts to something, and by extension so does mine. *I matter.*

The Rosary

'Thus graveyards are a way of keeping the dead handy but removed, dear but a little distant, gone but not forgotten.'

Thomas Lynch, *The Undertaking*

'Perhaps we need not grieve over the fact that half the original churchyards of Norwich (there were once sixty) cannot now be traced.'

R. H. Mottram, *If Stones Could Speak*

I have been walking up and down the rows, looking for a face I think I remember, one I'm sure I'll recognise when I see it. I must have spent whole days of my life searching in places like this, stupefied by the sheer profusion of the dead and their teeming memorials. I'm reminded of my son, aged six, as we drove past a graveyard with its massed ranks of headstones and white carved angels, saying in astonishment: *Look how many people have died.*

Dawdling like a tourist at the ruins. Distracted, too, by beauty and strangeness. Under a scaffold of winter trees, a broad flight of steps, slippery with leaves, connecting the older section of the cemetery with the new. The restless ground, heaving with the thirsty roots of lime, oak and poplar. A large gravelled plot split open lengthwise, as if to make way for the rising dead. A stone cross toppled and splayed like a shot bird. A birch sapling thrust up from the grave of someone who died aged seventy-seven and whose identity has been forgotten but whose stone bears the words: *Thou shalt come to thy grave in a full age like as a shock of corn cometh in his season.*

As I stand and stare, I hear a trundling sound, and a convulsive smoker's cough, and a man on a mobility scooter rounds the bend at speed and brakes sharply to greet me. What am I planning, he asks me – an angel, a dove? He wants black marble, carved in the shape of his Jack Russell. Nothing, I say, I want nothing. He's shocked. *Oh, but you must.*

On my second circuit, I catch sight of the face I've been looking for, and greet it like an old friend. The mason who worked this stone bust was a skilled craftsman, particularly good at texture: the cloth of the jacket creases realistically where the button pulls it, and if stone eyes could twinkle, these would. It was a quality piece of work, since defaced by the less accomplished nose-job it's had at some point; there's a blob of excess cement and a conspicuous line where the old stone meets the paler new. The monument is encompassed by railings and a skirt of brown leaves. Ivy sneaks up the pedestal, but has been clipped back so that the marble panels and their inscriptions can be seen:

> JOHN BARKER, STEAM CIRCUS PROPRIETOR,
> WHO WAS ACCIDENTALLY KILLED
> ON NORWICH CATTLE MARKET
> APRIL 12 1897 AGED 60 YEARS

> HAD HE ASKED US, THIS WE KNOW,
> WE SHOULD HAVE CRIED, O SPARE THIS BLOW,
> YES, WITH STREAMING TEARS SHOULD SAY,
> LORD, WE LOVE HIM, LET HIM STAY.

The delicacy of the sculpture-work, and the ornamental pillars and domed roof which shelter it, suggests a man of status and significance, someone worthy of public commemoration. If the Rosary is a city of the dead, then John Barker has a smart home in one of its better neighbourhoods. With his dignified bearing and patrician smile, he gives every appearance of belonging here among the illustrious sons of Norwich. His close neighbours are merchant bankers, members of Parliament and philanthropists, men of substance like Jeremiah Colman, founder of the mustard empire, James Sillett, painter of the Norwich School, and Corporal George Wilde, survivor of the Charge of the Light Brigade.

John Barker can hardly have expected to find himself in such established company. He didn't come from Norfolk, and his family had no roots here. He spent his entire adult life as a travelling showman, a man of no fixed abode. His origins are unclear; some said he was born in Kent, others Lincolnshire, or perhaps Ireland. Since his parents were also travelling people, perhaps it didn't matter much. Home was a horse-drawn caravan, and he was always on the move from town to town and from fair to fair. But although his itinerary took him all over England, and although most of his friends and business contacts were travellers, his livelihood depended on the people in the places where he pitched up: the officials he had to deal with, the locals he met on the street or in the pub, the punters who came along expecting the maximum thrills for their money. No doubt some places were more congenial than others. And by long tradition, Norwich was a city which embraced those whose lives did not conform to the usual pattern.

Steam, that everyday magic which made the Industrial Revolution, made John Barker too. He began by following in his father's footsteps, making a modest living from the same hand-cranked swings and dobbies. But he was a talented engineer, and one of the first to see the potential of new technology to drive bigger, faster and more exciting fairground rides. He went into business with his friend Henry Thurston, and they ploughed everything they had into developing a roundabout driven by steam engine. I've seen a grainy black-and-white photograph of it in a book of fairground history, with a caption noting that it was built by Tidman and Sons here in Norwich, and made its first appearance in 1896.

A few months later, John Barker was back, setting up for the fair which took place every Easter on Castle Hill. At three o'clock on the fatal afternoon, he and his carter were manoeuvring a number of trucks on a sloping street, when one of them overran the blocks positioned in front of the wheels. It collided with a trolley, and the two vehicles hurtled downhill, on a collision course with the living vans. In a desperate effort to avoid disaster, Barker stepped into the gap behind the trolley and caught hold of the brake, but at that moment the truck caught up and smashed into the back of the trolley, crushing him to death.

Today his face is untroubled, bathed in cold sunshine, and his benevolent gaze is fixed somewhere in the distance. I stand close and follow with my own eyes to see where it falls: somewhere out to the south-west, far beyond the perimeter fence, the quiet road of suburban houses, the tall gable and gothic tracery of the Jonathan Scott Primitive Methodist Chapel. All were familiar sights in his day, but they had no claim on him then and they don't seem to hold his interest now. He takes in the neon-green sign of the Holiday Inn, and the bright-yellow crane on a construction site beyond the busy ring road. Those who knew him in life chose to position him here after death, on rising ground and with a long view. The sculptor put a distant look in his eyes, a gaze which reaches further still, well beyond the city limits, to a low hill with a dark fuzz of winter trees, and the Tacolneston digital radio mast, hung with red lights.

The Scott Chapel has been sold off and converted to offices: Policy Direct Insurance, A2Z Travel, PFB Construction. Those old chapels, spacious and solidly constructed, can always find new uses when the faithful move on.

Religious non-conformism was part of the life of Norwich from at least the fourteenth century. On my way here today, I noticed that the pub I remembered as the Bridge House had acquired a very old new name: the Lollards' Pit. It stands on the site of a disused chalk pit, marked on an early map as 'the place where men are cus-tomablie burnt'. Countless heretics were executed there, and long after the killing ceased the pit was still considered an evil place. 'Many a saint of God has breathed his last beneath that white precipice,' wrote George Borrow. 'Many a grisly procession has advanced ... across the old bridge, towards the Lollards' Hole.' But the city moves on, and the horrors of the past are modulated. The new pub sign is a light-hearted depiction of two martyrs going up in a whoosh of flames, and cheery banners advertise real ales and a quiz night.

It will never be known how many met their deaths here. As a method of deterrence, it was not a great success. This remained a city of dissenters. 'Begin with Norwich,' said Elizabeth I when she gave orders to suppress the Puritans. But that bloody episode was no more effective than the last. Geographical remoteness had fostered a spirit of independence and self-determination. People did not like being told how to live their lives. 'Norfolk people do things different,' as the old maxim has it. This was not just contrariness for the sake of it, but a kind of confidence based on the prevailing realities of geography and economics. Norwich was outward-looking and well connected. Until the coming of the steam railway, it was quicker to travel to Amsterdam than to London, and the boats which went between here and continental Europe with their cargoes of worsted, tobacco, leather and timber also conveyed a traffic of ideas and culture. In this climate, attempts by the established church to enforce its authority were met with bitter resistance. The city's non-conformists – Unitarians, Methodists, Baptists, Congregationalists, Jews, atheists – possessed conviction and strength in numbers, and were not to be subjugated.

By the nineteenth century there was particularly strong resentment over the issue of burial and funerary ritual. The only licensed places of burial were the churchyards, and there was no alternative to the Church of England's burial rites. It presented a serious conflict of conscience for people who did not accept the established doctrine. Thomas Drummond, a retired minister, knew from experience the misery this could entail. On several occasions he had tried in vain to arrange a Christian burial for a child whose baptism had taken place in another tradition. In his retirement he decided to do something about it. His grand vision was for a new kind of burial ground, a dignified and beautiful place where any-one could be interred according to their own wishes and without compromising their religious beliefs. He bought a piece of land and persuaded local businessmen to invest in the scheme. Shares sold quickly in anticipation of a strong market and a good return.

Over the next twenty years, a similar vision would be realised in other cities in England, with the building of garden cemeteries such as Rusholme Road in Manchester and Abney Park in London. But Drummond was in the vanguard of this new move-ment, and he made an extraordinary personal investment in his plan. The Rosary opened in 1821, and his wife Anne Drummond was the first person to be buried here. She had already been dead and buried for two years, but her husband had her body exhumed from the churchyard and reinterred. It was a striking (and some said distasteful) public demonstration of his commitment to the project.

Take-up was slow in the early years, and the patience of his investors was tested. But by the middle of the century the urban population had exploded, and the bold project came of age. The city's churchyards were so overcrowded that their surfaces had risen high above street level, and worshippers on their way to ser-vice trod carefully to avoid displaced human bones. A drinking fountain near St John Maddermarket had to be sealed, because the water, with its unusually bright and sparkling quality, was said to be 'almost pure essence of churchyard'.

These congested and chaotic burial places were an open invita-tion to the grave-robber and the body-snatcher, and Drummond's spacious and well-regulated garden cemetery began to look like a more secure alternative. The Rosary became a desirable place of burial, attracting the custom of the city's wealthiest and most distinguished dead.

I first saw the Rosary in my early twenties, when I lived in Norwich for a while. I too was itinerant at the time, of no fixed abode. I came here from another temporary address 300 miles away to move in with the man I had met and fallen in love with that summer. There was no real plan. I packed a few possessions – a spare pair of jeans, a shirt or two, a dozen books – and threw the rest away. I made the grindingly slow train journey from rural mid-Wales to East Anglia, smoking my last pack of Benson & Hedges on the way and tossing my cigarette lighter into a platform bin at Peterborough. He met my train and we walked to our new quarters: a rented room in a large Victorian villa on Wroxham Road.

It was a house of cheerful chaos, where it was impossible to sit on any chair, put down a cup or take a bath without first clearing a space in the muddle of Stickle Bricks and smeared plates, books and babies' vests and the dog-ends of old joints. There was a vegetable garden completely overrun with nettles and bolted spinach. The couple we lived with were the warmest of people, friends rather than landlords. They were non-conformists too: what the tolerant neighbours with their sensible cars and neat hedges might have called hippies, or 'alternative types'. We supplemented our rental pittance with cooking and babysitting, learning as we went, so that by the time our own children came along it was second nature to cook up a thrifty stew from butterbeans and vegetable ends and spoon it into their small mouths.

Yesterday afternoon I stood in the stone gateway of that house, where I had not stood for twenty-five years. The gravel drive was tall with dockweed and willowherb. A half-eaten pizza and its box had been chucked in from the street and allowed to stay. One look at the house, though, was enough to tell me that they were still living there. The windowsills, peeled and rotting, were heaped with the same souvenirs – pebbles and fossils and pine cones – so familiar that I felt I could have picked through them and found the ones we brought back from our trip to the beach at Happisburgh in 1985.

Heavy curtains were drawn across all the windows, faded and torn, dangling from the rails in places. It looked to me as though they had been pulled across many years ago and not been opened since. The world had been shut out. Had my friends gone away and left the house empty, or were they living like shadows in those curtained interiors, just as they live in the screened and airless rooms of my memory? I felt a rush of gratitude when I thought of them, but it was shot through with apprehension. Neither they nor I had been good at keeping in touch, and a lot of life had happened to all of us since those days. I had come here longing to see them, to reclaim this sliver of the past, but it was hard to imagine those vibrant people in old age. Very likely they would have forgotten, or wouldn't want to be bothered. He could be quite fierce, I now remembered, and she was weary and pessimistic a lot of the time; weren't these both traits which tended to intensify over time? After knocking once and receiving no answer I walked away quickly, breathing with relief. There was an odd scraping sound which made me turn back briefly, but there was no sign of movement and I decided it must be a pigeon on the roof.

Wroxham Road is one of the main routes into Norwich. Unbroken streams of traffic are sucked along it into the city in the mornings and away again at night. My first week here, I answered an advert in the local paper and bought an old bicycle, rust held together with green paint, on which I rattled along in the gutter, harassed and hooted at, my Indian-print skirt hitched up to stop it catching in the wheel. Soon I learned less stressful ways on quieter roads, and my exploration of the city began. There were few hills to negotiate – it was shockingly flat – and since my gears were permanently jammed that was just as well. I would set off with a rucksack full of empty jars, which I'd take into the wholefoods shop on St Benedicts Street, where you filled them yourself from barrels of honey and peanut butter. I'd lock the bike to railings at St Peter Mancroft and wander round the market, or leave it somewhere on Tombland and spend a couple of hours in the cathedral.

After a time I ventured outside the city centre, cycling north to lie in the sun on Mousehold Heath, or west to snoop around the UEA campus and feed the ducks on the lake by the ziggurats. On one of these trips, testing an alternative route home, I discovered the Rosary, tucked away behind a quiet street on the edge of town. As I wheeled my bike past the Victorian chapel of rest I saw a little owl sitting on the porte-cochère, so perfectly still that at first I mistook it for one of the gargoyles perched there, expressions blurred smooth by 150 years of weather. It was the guardian and gatekeeper of this place, pretending now to be made of stone, but now launching into flight, rising on quick wingbeats over the rows of graves and looping in among the trees beyond.

No doubt there have been owls here for many hundreds of years. Graveyards have long memories. They remember what they were before they were annexed for human burial: fields, woods, open countryside. There are always vestiges of that earlier life: a hollow tree, a bit of ancient hedgerow, the seeds and spores of the species that once tenanted the place, long before the dead were drafted in. The Rosary was laid out on the site of a market garden, but before that it was open heathland, lying outside the bounds of the city. There are still survivors from that time: heather and gorse, humming with bees in summer; wood sorrel and Star of Bethlehem; reflexed stonecrop with its wonderful local name, 'prick-madam'. The graves are not as densely packed as in a municipal cemetery, and Drummond would be pleased to find that it has kept its park-like quality, its broad paths and glades, stands of hornbeam, beech and oak. In August the locals come blackberrying. I've seen woodpeckers, foxes, and muntjac deer rooting in the leaves for food.

With the new cemeteries came a more permissive attitude towards the design of memorials, and there are some flamboyant examples here. The mausoleum of Emanuel Cooper has a trapezoidal doorway where he used to sit smoking his pipe on Sunday afternoons, trying out the place, enjoying the view. He moved indoors long ago, and an immense old chain and padlock now secure the surrounding railings: someone is taking no risks. A little further uphill, Jeremiah Cozens of Sprowston is commemorated with a sarcophagus of cast iron, supported on lion's paws complete with monstrous claws and curls of hair. At either end, an iron ring is held in the mouth of a lion, and the piece is crowned with a cold conflagration of iron flames. Wealth and privilege are as conspicuous in death as they were in life. Between the grand tombs of the rich and powerful, simpler stones recall those whose names are mostly forgotten. The names themselves are in many cases improbable to the modern ear: Ephraim Grice, Fanny Pigg, Theodore Madge, Barzillai Baldwin, Elijah Willgrass.

John Barker's own plain and timeless name has lapsed into obscurity. But on the day of his funeral, thousands of mourners lined the route of the cortege, and followed the coffin to the burial place, in rain so relentless and torrential that they still talked about it years afterwards. A grand funeral procession was a real entertainment at that time, but the crowds were exceptional even so. In one of the eulogies delivered that day, he was given the appellation 'Father of the Fair'. He may have been known by this title in life, or it may have been one of those flashes of rhetorical brilliance which catch the mood of the moment. Either way, he was certainly a pioneer in his field, one of those who brought the modern-day fair into being. And he seems to have been a father figure in another sense too: a man known among fairground people for his kindness and generosity, 'one to whom no appeal in any genuine case of need was ever made in vain', as the speaker put it. The kind of man who would not stop to consider his own safety, but would throw himself between a runaway truck and a living van with women and children inside.

The outpouring of grief over his death seems extraordinary, given that he was not a local man, and that he spent his life on the move. But it was that itinerant lifestyle, and the need to protect it, that made his name. He was not only a lifelong traveller, but one of the founders of a movement to defend the rights of travelling people, at a time when they were threatened in the name of social reform. The Showmen's Guild of Great Britain, which still exists today, evolved from an earlier body, formed in a hurry, by John Barker and half a dozen of his contemporaries. A decade later, in honour of the part he played, it was that body – the United Kingdom Showman and Van Dwellers' Association – which raised the money to pay for this monument. Within a fortnight of his death, members had clubbed together to raise £50, and had commissioned a sculptor to come up with a design.

Travelling people have always had a bad press. In my own child-hood, when the Statutes Fair came to town each autumn, there were muttered warnings about the disreputable and dangerous characters who came with it. They lived by different rules, people said, and although they were 'not proper Romanies' they had their own language and codes of behaviour. There were van-dwellers not only at fairgrounds but also wherever there were roadworks; the ugliness of torn-up ground and heaped gravel was softened by a few tokens of domesticity – a flowery curtain, a grubby box of Cornflakes on the sill – glimpsed on the verge where the diggers and rollers were parked up for the night. And there was the gypsy site on waste ground at the far edge of town, which was the subject of sporadic outbreaks of bitter complaint in the local papers.

In its own time, the Association strove hard for a different image. A photograph of the founders shows a line-up of sober, respectable figures with smart suits and collars, chains of office, jewelled tie-pins. Theirs was a brotherhood born out of urgent necessity, formed hurriedly to fight a desperate battle to keep their way of life from extinction. To have any chance of success it needed to sway public opinion, and that started with the right look. The 1880s had seen a growing crusade amongst politicians and church-men to 'reform' and 'educate' travelling people, which in practice meant preventing them from travelling and forcing them to settle in one place like everyone else. The Moveable Dwellings Bill of 1888 required each dwelling to be officially registered, and granted powers to local authority officers to enter unannounced, on any day and at any time, in order to inspect it for sanitation, health and 'moral irregularities'. The bill was sponsored by the evangelist and social reformer George Smith of Coalville, who characterised van-dwellers as 'dregs of society, that will one day put a stop to the work of civilisation, and bring to an end the advance in arts, science, law and commerce that have been making such rapid strides in the country'. Unsurprisingly, he was loathed and despised among fairground people, who recognised the bill as a declaration of war, an effort to annihilate them. On one occasion, after turning up at Birmingham Onion Fair intent on preaching to them about the errors of their ways and converting them to his own, Smith was chased off the platform and through the streets to the bank of the canal, where he had to be rescued by the local police.

Meanwhile, John Barker and other leading showmen were organising. They held a meeting, at which they decided to band together to protect and safeguard the interests of their community. They distributed pamphlets at fairs and shows, gathered thousands of signatures on a petition, lobbied members of Parliament and secured the support of some leading politicians, clergymen and lawyers. George Smith was seen off, and the Moveable Dwellings Bill defeated. The privacy of a mobile home was defended, at least for the time being.

Sitting here now, close to dusk, I can hear the dirge of rush-hour traffic on the ring road. This place seems carved out of time, and holds its own deep stillness; there's a sweet smell of cold earth and wood smoke, and the clumps of early snowdrops glow greenish-white as the light around them fades. The man on the mobility scooter has gone, and there's only the occasional flicker of movement between the trees as someone takes this peaceful shortcut towards the warmth of home. A skein of geese flies over in silence.

We are all travellers. If John Barker stepped down from his podium right now, and strode away along the path, I would feel no surprise at all.

However juicy the news, local papers hold it in proportion. A grisly death and a spectacular funeral must jostle for position with all the other stories of the day. Life in Norfolk that week in 1897 was the usual mix, and the report from the Rosary takes its place among accounts of hooliganism ('Desperate affray in Wymondham Market-Place – Policeman assaulted'), binge-drinking ('A Fatal Wager – Quart of Whisky at a draught'), and crime ('Sacrilege in Norwich: St Philip's Church "cracked" and offertory boxes forced'). On the other hand, the Spring Flower Show is on; subscriptions are being collected towards the forthcoming Diamond Jubilee celebrations; and there's a largely favourable review of a production of *Sweet Lavender* by the Norwich Thespians. The report of the funeral concludes with an announcement which must have cheered the spirits of pleasure-seekers up and down the land: 'We are asked to state that the business which the late Mr Barker so successfully conducted will continue to be carried on by his widow and family.'

Since then, Barkers Amusements has been passed down through the generations and is still going strong, touring the fairgrounds of England with its dodgems, waltzers, Fun House and Ghost Train. They may well have come with 'the Statchits' to my hometown when I was a child, where in the first week of October the rides and stalls were set up in and around the old marketplace, making everything exhilaratingly different for a few days. To look down from the top of the Big Wheel on those streets and shops and brewery yards was to feel braver and freer than usual, to know you could leave it behind if you chose to. It was a revelation, and like all wisdom it had to be learned over time. Until the age of seven or eight, your mother would collect you from school and take you straight there, where you had to make do with a little train running its tame circle in broad daylight; if you were quick enough, you got to sit in the engine and pull a whistle every now and then. Afterwards there would be the agonising choice between candyfloss and toffee apple, which you made in the knowledge that the candyfloss would get stuck in your hair, and that the apple would be brown and mushy inside and that you'd be expected to eat it nonetheless. But to see the fair for the first time after dark was to glimpse what it was really about; and to reach an age where you were allowed to go without parental supervision, perhaps at eleven or twelve, was a rite of passage in which you took possession of its giddy hedonism, its reckless and sensuous delights. No doubt the nineteenth-century children of Norwich experienced something similar.

The cattle market, the site of the Easter fair where John Barker was setting up his steam circus on the day he died, was razed long ago and replaced with a shopping mall. The road layout has changed, and the streets and buildings remember nothing of him. Even in the immediate aftermath, no mention was made of him at the regular meetings of the markets committee. A fortnight after his spectacular funeral, permission is again granted for his steam roundabout to be placed on the Bull Ring in exchange for a payment of ten pounds, but the item is passed without comment. Complaints are heard against a preacher and a man playing the banjo, causing obstruction and annoyance on market days. There is much ponderous discussion of tramways, of cow and calf railings, of weights and measures and cleansing contracts. The business of the market and its weekly affairs runs on as if nothing has happened.

The inquest recorded a verdict of accidental death, and the coroner summed up with a warning on 'the desirability where there is a decline in the ground to draw up the waggons at an angle with the decline'. It was after all a very ordinary calamity. The brisk entry in the register includes a note of the various fees and disbursements, which are totted up to £4 3s. 8d. As I turned the pages of the register this morning, I was reminded that although death rolls on inexorably through the centuries, and is in its essentials pure and immutable, the ways in which people die change over time. In 1890s Norfolk, folk toppled out of waggonettes, were crushed by coal trucks, set themselves alight with paraffin lamps, plunged from wherries. Josiah Woodrow died when he fell into a copper of boiling beer. Frederick Brown fell on the fork of a threshing machine. Alice Puttock, fifteen years old, tumbled through an open factory doorway into the River Wensum (and her inquest incurred an extra five shillings 'river fee'). Death strikes indiscriminately in leisure and at work; in the same year in which the Father of the Fair met his end, Samuel Coy was fatally injured by a fall from a swinging boat.

How conscientious we are in our attempt to inquire of death, especially when it arrives suddenly and unexpectedly. The precision of these official sentences, the detail of place and time, the scrupulous penmanship. The care with which these books were kept up to date, and have since been archived and curated, though the wherry was broken up for scrap and the factory with its dangerous trapdoor closed down a hundred years ago. John Barker's was just one of many sudden deaths that year, and by no means the most remarkable. In some cases, the means of death is so peculiar that it stays in the mind long after closing the register and walking out of the building. When I shut my eyes tonight, I think I will still see an impression, like a faded photograph, of the final inexplicable seconds in the life of William Bloomfield Brett, aged forty-nine. He pauses with his lit spill for a moment, before reaching out and touching it to the tap on the tank of ether.

After Wroxham Road, and the windows blanked out with tattered curtains, I drove a mile or two to look at another of my old addresses, a rented flat over a corner shop. I liked living there. It was very convenient to be able to climb out of bed and wander down in bare feet to buy milk. I recall the time when we bought our very first piece of furniture – a red kitchen stool from a junk shop – and conveyed it home lashed to the back of a bicycle. It was a snowy winter, and we couldn't afford to switch on the heating, but there was always a roaring fire at the cosy old pub just down the road.

When I returned, the shop had gone and the flats had been rebuilt. It was difficult to reconcile what I remembered with what I was looking at now. It wasn't until I gave up, mooched round the corner and approached the Red Lion that I experienced a stab of recognition. When I peered in at the window, I sensed a near-forgotten taste in my mouth. I interrogated it a moment and recognised it as the taste of rum and blackcurrant cordial. Rum-and-black, one of the drinks of my youth, a cheap nip of sweetness and warmth to keep out the chill of damp rooms, essay deadlines and leaking boots.

Eagerly I pushed open the door, half-expecting to catch my old self sitting by the fire with a glass in my hand. But the taste evaporated instantly. The pub was now fitted out as a restaurant. The old settles were gone, replaced by rows of tables set for dinner. The only customers were a man and his teenage son, sitting tensely at one of the tables with their pints, trying not to mess up the place settings. But the staff were expecting a busy night: as I hesitated in the doorway, a massive joint of lamb was carried through from the kitchen and wedged on the hotplate behind glass. In the chimney corner where we used to sit, the hearth gaped empty except for the iron fire-tools displayed on its swept tiles like museum exhibits. Above the mantelpiece, with its framed menu and *Thank You for Not Smoking* sign, hung the stone face of a lion with a ring in its mouth, a dead spit of the one on Jeremiah Cozens' tomb at the Rosary.

Perched disapprovingly on a dining chair with a glass of Adnams, I flicked through the fairground history book and looked again at the black-and-white photograph of John Barker's circular steam switchback. The cars were designed in the style of Venetian gondolas, each one individually scrolled and gilded, an angel head and wings at the back and a carved relief of a dragon at the front. There were two hills in the track, with a deep drop between them, and a walkway where spectators could stand. *Barker & Thurston*, read the fancy lettering at the top of the spinning frame. According to the caption, it was lit with arc lamps and the music was supplied by an 87-key Gavioli barrel organ. It must have been a wildly glamorous sight, even for the passers-by who could only afford to watch.

When these new contraptions started to appear on fairgrounds, they were greeted with something close to hysteria. Thrill-seekers frequently had to be treated for fainting fits and weak hearts afterwards. One eyewitness wrote breathlessly of 'a roundabout of huge proportions ... whirled about with such impetuosity, that the wonder is the daring riders are not shot off like cannon ball, and driven half way into next month'. The first appearance of his steam circus at Tombland Fair in 1896 drew such crowds that John Barker began looking for a way to extend the season into winter. He hit on an enterprising solution: he would hire the Agricultural Hall and install it there. The hall had been used for entertainments before: it had hosted magic-lantern shows, and the great Blondin had once walked a tightrope slung between the upper balconies with a trumpeter on his back. Still, this was an ambitious venture. Part of the glass roof had to be removed and replaced with a sheet of iron with a hole cut in the centre to accommodate the chimney from the steam engine. But the risk paid off. There were blinding snowstorms and heavy drifting all over East Anglia that winter, but the Agricultural Hall glowed with music and coloured lights. No wonder Norwich took John Barker to its heart.

There's almost nothing left of him but his stone likeness among the silent mansions of the Rosary. His steam switchback was broken up long ago. Only the barrel organ is still going strong, installed in a set of Golden Gallopers and touring the fairs and markets of England. One day, when I'm visiting some town or other, crossing a square full of shoppers and *Big Issue* sellers, I might walk past those Gallopers without really noticing them. But there's a chance

I'll catch the unmistakeable wheezy tones of 'Daisy Bell' or 'Down at the Old Bull and Bush', one of the same tunes John Barker whistled along to as he stood with a sooty rag in his hand and watched the fancy gondolas on their circuit, at the height of his powers, in that golden winter of 1896.

Not far from John Barker's handsome statue is a simple white headstone commemorating Ralph Hale Mottram, author and Lord Mayor of Norwich, along with his wife and two of his children. (The inscription for the third has already been added, but with the death date yet to be completed.) 'I knew, when I was four years old, exactly where I would be buried,' Mottram once said. All his life he felt a strong sense of belonging, not only to Norwich but also to the Rosary itself. Burial is sometimes spoken of as a kind of homecoming: a return not just to the earth, the common source and destination for us all, but to a particular plot, a place of personal significance.

If this was John Barker's homecoming, it was as appropriate as any other. He could have died in any town in England, but chance and an accident of death brought him here and Norwich took him in. And a necropolis like the Rosary – a shadow-city, complete with all its trappings of wealth and status, all its many shades of belonging – is bound to acquire over time a mixed and disparate population. Even the muntjac deer that root in the leaf-litter between the graves originated in south-east Asia. And *Athene noctua*, the little owl which was introduced into Britain for the first time when John Barker was in his middle years, can perch on the chapel of rest in this Norfolk cemetery and look just as local as if it were struck from flint.

Ruin

The ruinous state of graveyards and the loss of old memorials can be very disturbing to the living, though perhaps it's not exactly the loss of them but the sight of them in a dilapidated condition that provokes anxiety and shame. Occasionally there is a tomb or mausoleum which has some specific heritage value, and some do gain the status of listed monuments. But these feelings of dismay are not really to do with rare examples of funerary architecture. Regardless of special merit or famous historical association, the decay we see around us in these places confronts the living with a sense of disgrace: a collective failure to remember the dead, to respect them as we should. Deliberate desecration has the power to outrage and even terrify, but the dispassionate vandalism of weather and time is more troubling still, because it is inexorable, a kind of endless attrition.

On the other hand, a graveyard in a state of beautiful ruin can become a tourist attraction. In Abney Park I once saw a couple posing for their wedding photographs among the crumbling tombs and toppled angels. 'Ruin lust' is a defining feature of Romanticism; poets and painters of the eighteenth and nineteenth centuries loved to depict the brokenness of our human things. The image of the village churchyard with its decaying stonework was already a cliché by 1850. Nevertheless, it still has us in its grip. Rose Macaulay identifies this as the expression of an innate human paradox: what she calls 'the ruin-drama staged perpetually in the human imagination, half of whose desire is to build up, while the other half smashes and levels to the earth'. From infancy on, we are all makers, and we are all destroyers.

I see the broken and erased state of the tombs around me here not as decorative, and not as a necessary evil, but as exact and perfectly functional. The inevitability of natural processes – rain, frost, root-heave, fox-dig – are built into the system. They are part of the purpose, intrinsic to the meaning of the graveyard: life is fleeting; the greatest among us, like the least, will die. Even the motif of the hourglass, however skilfully carved in stone, will be rubbed out by the years. The mason knows this, and operates in partnership with these processes. Together they construct a model demonstrating how time works.

VI

The graveyard in autumn. Bunched knots of rowan-
berries, prematurely festive in the not-quite
dusk, and the slip and grit of them underfoot.
Such profusion, such excess! Then the first frost,
and a party of starlings that strip the tree to
the bone.

St Agnes of Blean

'So passeth, in the passing of a day,
Of mortall life the leafe, the bud, the flowre'

Edmund Spenser, 'The Faerie Queene'

'There are never in nature two beings which are precisely alike.'

Gottfried Leibniz, *Discourse on Metaphysics*

In Dane John Gardens in Canterbury there was a fuzz of new buds on the lime trees, and children playing on the Roman burial mound. This park, like so many others, had a previous life as a cemetery, and has not forgotten it. It has a double character, equivocating between recreation and memorial. The family picnic, the teenagers huddled over a spliff, the scooters, buggies and bikes. Metal plaques on the benches calling to mind 'Alderman Smith Temple, 1896–1959', 'Muriel Foad, who loved this place', 'Ben, a brother and a friend', or simply 'Grandad'.

As I meandered through that not-quite graveyard, where the past has been landscaped and laid out with rose beds, fountains and a bandstand, I was trying to catch hold of my own memories and drag them to the surface. Those I had were vivid but isolated, lacking in context. I spent my student years in this town, but that time, and the self who lived it, felt remote and unlikely. Could she really have been me? Where was she now? It occurred to me as a genuine possibility that I might at any moment catch sight of her. Life, under such a conscious effort of remembering, sometimes resembles a series of clumsy jump-cuts rather than one continuous narrative. I hardly seemed to know this place at all; most of what I thought I knew turned out to be wrong. All I had was this collection of scattered moments which seemed, as I thought of them now, luminous with freshness and youth. It was not so much events I was recalling but that feeling of freshness itself.

I stopped under the avenue of limes and concentrated hard. Somewhere in this city was a pub I used to frequent, where I first played bar billiards and was surprised to find I was good at it. They served a type of farm cider so dry that drinking it made you thirsty. Where was that pub and what was it called? I gathered a group of friends there on my nineteenth birthday; I thought I had a photograph of this occasion, but I hadn't been able to find it and I was beginning to wonder whether it ever existed. But I clearly remembered the jeans and red shirt I was wearing that night.

I recalled too the smell and taste of the shepherd's pies we used to eat on Sundays, at another pub in another part of town. We loved them because they were cheap and hearty and reminded us of the proper food of home. They were served in thick brown terracotta bowls, scratched white inside, and there were sticky bottles of Worcester sauce on the tables.

Then there was the room I rented in 1982: an attic room with a pink and brown patchwork quilt on the bed. Visits from my boyfriend were monitored by my landlord, an unsmiling man, very thin and intense, who liked to lecture me on politics over breakfast. It was the time of the Falklands War, and his favourite word was 'escalation'. I lay awake at night with the radio turned down low and pressed to my ear in case there was any news. Even if I wished to find that house again, I couldn't. I remember the boiled smell of the hallway, the lumpy weight of the quilt, the turn-and-a-half you had to make with the key, but none of the useful facts like the name of the street or whether the trains I could hear in the early mornings were pulling out of Canterbury East or Canterbury West.

This shocking amnesia must mean I never knew the place well. Apart from the brief and unhappy time in the attic room, I never made the city my home or entered properly into its society. The university campus is on a hill to the north, and we made all our own entertainments up there and in the seaside bedsits and squats of Herne Bay and Margate. It wasn't until my final year, when the tight cocoon of student life was thinning and cracking, that I began to notice at last that I was located in a *somewhere* which could be explored. I started to make small solitary forays into that somewhere, starting with the church of St Cosmus and St Damian in the Blean, where I idled my way round the churchyard, reading the gravestones, distracted from worrying about my own future by the two mysteries I found there. It was less than a mile from campus, along an ancient footpath, a section of the old salt road linking the city of Canterbury with Whitstable and the salt marshes of Seasalter. But that little distance was a shortcut between one set of realities and another. Walking that path was like taking brief excursions out of my self and into the world.

How it started is one of those bright but deracinated memories. After a fortnight of procrastination I have been at my desk all night, chewing Pro Plus and trying to write an extended essay on Leibniz's Law of Identicals. It is painfully apparent that I have missed a crucial lecture on the subject. At six a.m., I shuffle despairingly through what I've managed to cobble together, unfold myself from the chair and go to lean on the windowsill. Outside, everything is smoky with early morning light. I feel as if I'm seeing the familiar view for the first time, in particular the footpath which leads off-campus, running parallel with the road at first and then veering away between woods on one side and open fields on the other. No time now – I have another 3,000 words to write by lunchtime – but later, I promise myself, I will walk that path.

In the churchyard the ground is sodden and the sky racing. Floral tributes have been swiped by the wind and scattered. I pick up a square of card on a green plastic spike: *Missing you still*. A slab of limestone is propped wearily over the grave of Edward and

Frances Gibbs. On the stone of Stephen Gibbs, lichen has flared up brilliantly from the base in a pattern of green flames, almost engulfing his name and dates.

When I unlatch the door of the church, the wind pushes past me and races in, sweeping the welcome leaflets off the table and throwing them down. It takes an effort to heave the door shut. The two saints in their stained-glass window are eerily animated by the threshing shadows of the trees outside. There's a huge block of oasis on the sill, and bunches of yellow and white carnations in a bucket beneath, along with stems of the pussy-willow I saw in the hedges as I walked here, retracing my steps of thirty years ago. The wind thunders around on all sides, deepening the sense of stillness in this place. We are only four miles from the sea, and it's like being in the cabin of a boat at anchor, closed in by the weather, waiting for the storm to pass.

The saints flicker in their spandrels of coloured glass. Damian shakes his mortar and pestle, Cosmus holds a golden vessel of salve or unguent which flashes with light in his hands. These two enigmatic figures fascinated me from the first time I approached the churchyard gate and read their names on the noticeboard. I tried the door and was surprised to find it unlocked. A set of notes in a plastic sleeve told me that they were twins, both physicians, who lived and practised in the Roman province of Syria in the third century. A number of miraculous healings are attributed to them, including a fantastic surgical procedure in which they amputated the ulcerated leg of a white patient and replaced it by grafting on the leg of a dead Ethiopian. They refused to take payment for their services, spurning the profit motive in favour of religious principles of charity and poverty, and attracting the grateful population to the Christian faith by this witness. Under the persecution of Diocletian they were arrested and tortured, and when they refused to recant they were executed, along with their three brothers. I have since seen an exquisitely gruesome painting of their martyrdom by Fra Angelico, showing three of the brothers bloody and decapitated on the ground while the remaining two kneel blind-folded and await their turn.

Their wild tale sounds a very long way from this corner of Kent, with its quiet flint church and the green, sunlit path that brought me here. But it is the same path that brought them here too: the path trodden by a group of monks in 598, accompanying Augustine on his mission from Rome to convert the Anglo-Saxons to Christianity and become the first Archbishop of Canterbury. According to legend, the monks stopped at this spot for a time, perhaps making use of whatever was left of the Roman villa that once stood on this site. They set up a shrine, and dedicated it to the twins, who were two of their most revered saints.

The story of Cosmus and Damian was the first mystery. The second was the legend of Agnes Gibbs, granddaughter of Stephen whose headstone is consumed with green fire. I can't remember how I first encountered it – that's the nature of legends – but it has stayed with me all the years since. One night in 1850, two men met in this churchyard and carried out a secret burial. One of the men was the vicar, and the other the father of the dead child he had carried here from his home in the village. The child was two years old, but she had hardly grown at all since birth and was small enough to be wrapped in a pillowcase. The two men worked together by the light of a lantern to dig a small grave – no one knows where exactly, but perhaps not far from where I'm standing, close to the east wall of the church where the Gibbs family graves are. The father stood with his head bowed, and the vicar said the usual words: *We brought nothing into this world, and it is certain we can carry nothing out. The Lord gave, and the Lord hath taken away.*

If it wasn't the funeral they'd have wanted, William Gibbs must have thought it was the best they could do. His daughter Agnes had become such an object of curiosity that after her sudden death he had been advised to act quickly and discreetly. If they had buried her by daylight and marked the place with a stone, her body might have been exhumed and stolen by grave-robbers, perhaps hoping to sell her on to some unscrupulous showman ready to cash in on their misfortune.

There was a rumour on campus that the church was haunted, and I remember a rowdy party of us walking out there at night with torches but turning back when someone claimed they saw a figure between the trees and someone else became hysterical.

It is a lonely sight, circled by tall trees but isolated, forsaken by its village when the salt road fell out of use. In the fifteenth century, when the trade in herring and oysters was booming, a new route was forged between city and coast: a track which had the advantage of running close to a brook where people and horses could drink. A wealthy landowner left a bequest of 100 marks to improve the new track into 'an horse way for fysshe wyves', and gradually the old road was abandoned. Houses were built along the horse way, and the village shifted west. The church was stranded.

The village itself was little more than a backwater, a place to break the journey. At the turn of the eighteenth century, the historian Edward Hasted wrote that it was 'situated in a wild country, enveloped with woods, having much rough and poor land in it, and the inhabitants are in general like the soil, equally poor and rough'. By the time Agnes was born fifty years later the railway was pushing its way into rural Kent, but to the people of Blean, London would still have felt so remote it might as well have been New York. The news that the youngest Gibbs child was to be taken there, summoned by royalty, must surely have been electrifying. The legend tells that the Duchess of Kent had her brought to court so that she could see her with her own eyes and have her examined by the royal doctors. Once there, she was swept up into London society and became a sensation. She was known as 'the Fairy Queen', and her short life was one glamorous round of parties, shows and introductions.

In the parish records, there are many lives so sliver-thin that there is no time even for baptism. Agnes is more substantial. She is named, she takes her place as one of eleven children born to William and Sarah, and she survives for nineteen months. Her birth and death are properly certificated, the cause of death recorded as 'teething'. But these slender facts are all I've seen. My efforts to find out more have come to nothing. It seems there are no news reports, no correspondence, no surviving account of her visit to the duchess, no diary entry or note in the margin. Local people know the story, and it's recounted in a couple of sentences on the parish website, but no one can tell me any more.

I've often wondered how the infant daughter of a farmer from a small village in Kent could possibly have come to the attention of the royal household, though it is true that the nineteenth century was a time of intense public fascination with bodies and physical difference, and that royalty had always been particularly suscepti- ble. The tradition of keeping court dwarves may have died out, but the royal infatuation with smallness had not. Tom Thumb and Lavinia Warren were presented to Queen Victoria three times, and as late as 1912, Anita the Living Doll ('Age 30 years. Height, 26 inches. Perfect in Figure, Face and Form.') was brought before King George and Queen Mary, who expressed 'their delight and aston- ishment at seeing so Tiny, Intellectual, and Perfect a Little Lady'. A quotation like this represented a powerful asset to Anita's pro- moter, just like the royal coat of arms and the words 'By Appointment' on a box of Weetabix or a jar of golden syrup. But there is no record of Agnes receiving any such stamp of approval.

In Middle English, the word 'legende' meant 'story of a saint's life'. Such a story began with documented fact, but over time a wealth of additional narrative material developed around it, includ- ing miracles. There is no miraculous element in the legend of Agnes Gibbs – she was not cured, and she died before her second birthday – but in other ways her story seems as unlikely and as difficult to authenticate as the story of Damian and Cosmus. It must have been passed down through successive generations of villagers, but there seems to be nothing to lend it substance. It's like shaking a locked box, and wondering whether the faint rattle you hear is anything more than dust.

In the end, I find the key to the locked box, tucked between the pages of a nineteenth-century book called *Giants and Dwarfs* by Edward J. Wood. The book is a compilation of curious, bizarre and frequently troubling anecdotes, mixed with material transcribed directly from handbills and newspaper reports: 'The Marquis of Lilliput, one-fourth the size of life'; 'Chang, the Great Chinese Giant'; 'Dwarf and Pig-Faced Lady'; 'the Friesland Phenomenon' (twenty-eight inches high, and dressed up as a Dutch burgomaster, then an admiral, then a barrister in wig and gown).

One such transcript, from a handbill dated August 1850, provides me with the first tangible evidence that the legend of Agnes of Blean has some basis in fact:

> The Fairy Queen, now exhibiting at *Market Hill, High Street, Woolwich* [these words written in], acknowledged to be the smallest living child in the world. Two years old, sixteen inches high, and weighs only four pounds. Daughter of W. Gibbs, farmer, of Blean, Canterbury. Has been exhibited at the University College, London, before 500 medical gentlemen; has also had the honour of attending many private parties &c, at the residences of nobility, who have been astonished and delighted with her graceful manners, beauty of form, and lively disposition.

In fact Agnes was only eighteen months old when the handbill was posted, and she cannot possibly have weighed as little as four pounds; but exaggeration is the stock-in-trade of the showman. Neither are graceful manners common in infants of eighteen months. I wonder what sleight of hand was used to make her appear older and more sophisticated.

Wood goes on to mention a portrait of the Fairy Queen and her mother. It was published in the *Illustrated London News*, and copies were sold to audience members for a shilling each. In a state of excitement I track it down, but any hopes of catching a glimpse of Agnes are quickly dashed. It's an engraving by an unknown artist, showing a woman in a dark dress and frilled bonnet, her expression blank and generic. But she is positively lifelike compared with the small figure she holds in her left hand. The child is nothing more than a sketched outline, with some rudimentary shading to suggest the folds of a miniature crinoline, and face and hair hasty and approximate. Some other, unremarkable portrait has been taken and recycled, whatever was in the woman's hand excised, and the child drawn in crudely in its place. Nothing special, but it would do.

The most remarkable thing about this image, though, is not the way it looks but the fact that it is posthumous. It's dated May 1851, eight months after Agnes's death was certified and her name entered in the burial register for St Cosmus and St Damian. The picture illustrates a piece about her latest show:

> On Saturday we had the pleasure of paying a visit to one of the tiniest members of humanity who have ever taken up their abode in this great city. The young lady is at present thirteen months old, but in spite of her advanced age she only stands sixteen inches in height, and on going on to scale her weight is not more than five pounds – that is, she is about one-half the size and weight of a new-born infant, and all this with the utmost regularity of limb and feature.

She has gained a pound in weight, and yet her age has slipped, somehow, from two years to thirteen months. And suddenly it all makes sense. Her death created no interruption at all to the hiring of venues, the printing of handbills, the purchase of advertising space, because the Fairy Queen is not Agnes Gibbs, or any other individual child, but a brand. One little girl dies; she is replaced by another. The show goes on, the profits keep rolling in, the promoter is still in pocket and the punter none the wiser. The same is true of all those Fat Ladies, Jungle Boys and Living Skeletons. The whole freak-show business is a hall of mirrors, of endless duplication and illusion.

The sole function of the handbill and the newspaper advert is hype. Wood himself, writing in 1868, describes such material as 'professional puffs', and cautions his readers 'at once to lay in a store of salt, a grain of which he may take with advantage after reading each one of the following pages'. The lecture theatre, the throng of medical men, the glamorous parties: all fiction. Her appearance in Woolwich High Street was a shop-window show, installed very simply and at minimal expense in temporary premises standing empty between one lease and the next. The showman stood on a box on the pavement and spieled for passing trade. Success will have depended less on Agnes and her accomplishments than on the showman's ability to invent a good story and tell it well. If he could get a little crowd to stop and listen, he was halfway there. Shows like this had sprung up all over the city in recent years, cashing in on the public's insatiable taste for looking at unusual bodies. One showman wrote of his career: 'I have exhibited some curios things, and in some very curios places, every place imaginable, if there was any people about, place and space being no object. I have exhibited novelties in gateways, backyards, basements.'

Here in the churchyard, the storm has blown itself out, and the grass is steaming in the sun. Wet leaves plastered to the noticeboard. Under the yew, a forlorn pair of black underpants.

Legends are typically two-dimensional: strong on narrative but light on motivation. I'm curious to know what Agnes's parents hoped to get out of taking such a young child all the way to London. Were they hoping for a diagnosis, or assurances that their daughter's condition would change with time? Or were they persuaded by some more worldly acquaintance that there was money to be made in the new entertainment industry? Times were hard that year, with low crop prices and farmers driven to the brink; it may have looked like an answer to a desperate problem. Perhaps the link was made by an ambitious local man who decided to try his hand in the big city, and saw Agnes as his ticket to that new life. Or perhaps another Fairy Queen had unexpectedly grown too much, or her parents had changed their minds and withdrawn her, and the promoter was scouting around for a replacement. Agnes's story is actually the story of an unknown number of children, a series of separate individuals like the figures painted inside a zoetrope in a Victorian toyshop. Spin the cylinder, and through the slots all the little girls merge and become one girl, standing on the palm of her mother's hand.

Agnes died at nineteen months, before the development of the 'cognitive self' and the onset of autobiographical memory. Had she lived into adulthood, she would have been unable to recollect those early experiences: the journey to London, the shows, the audiences. In theory her career might have continued; Lavinia Warren went on performing until she died in her seventies. But most child acts lasted two or three years at best. This was a ruthless industry which chewed them up and spat them out. Promoters scrambled to outdo one another, introducing ever more sensational spectacles. The Fairy Queen was relatively tame, and the advertising material was written to appeal to an audience too squeamish for some of the most popular shows of the time. There were the Aztecs, a 'dwarfish and idiotic' brother and sister, said to be the only surviving members of a lost race rescued from a temple in Iximaya, where they were found squatting on the altar as objects of veneration. (An investigation found that this was all a fiction, and that they had been brought here by a Spanish trader who tricked the mother by offering to take them to New York for medical treatment, and promptly sold them on to an American showman.) Then there was the What-is-it?, a creature of indeterminate species who barked and mewed and roared, and capered about imitating a toad, a fly and a monkey. (Between shows at the Egyptian Hall in Piccadilly, an audience member sneaked backstage and uncovered the deception: the What-is-it? was nothing more exotic than a deformed child. He was promptly abandoned by his promoter, and died weeks later.)

Not until fifty years after Agnes's death was legislation passed prohibiting the showing of children under the age of ten for profit. Even then there were frequent breaches of the law. One court case in 1895 ended in a verdict of manslaughter against the parents of an infant, eight months old. They pleaded that they had only agreed to exhibit their daughter as a freak because her father had been dismissed from his job and they felt 'they had better do so rather than starve'.

I'm thinking of following the example of those Roman pilgrims and building a shrine here in the churchyard of St Cosmus and St Damian. After all, I have been a pilgrim of sorts here myself. I would dedicate it to Agnes of Blean, who should in my view be regarded as a kind of saint. This would be entirely in keeping with the tradition that existed in the early years of Christianity, when the title of saint was much more freely applied, and came about through local veneration rather than centralised legal process. No need to argue over whether her death qualifies as a martyrdom. It seems to me remarkable that someone who lived such a very short life has continued to matter to the people who live in the place where she once lived; her story has survived the almost two hundred years since her death, if only in the form of a misleading fragment. The making of a shrine would simply build on that vestigial survival. It would stand as a defence against amnesia, because human beings forget so much and the remembering we do is often wrong.

What to put in it? A statue would be traditional, and it is quite usual for it to be a generic representation, which is just as well since all we have to go on is the faked picture in the *Illustrated London News*. Or it could be a relic of some kind – a miniature finger-bone, perhaps – though I'd have to borrow one from someone else as the location of her grave is unknown, but this too would be customary. I shall build my shrine near the boundary fence, beside the old salt road. When joggers and cyclists and students from my old halls of residence pass by, they will pause here and think of Agnes of Blean, patron saint of the expendable, whose short and insignificant story is salutary and ought not to be forgotten. No record of any miracle is yet attributed to her name. But legends are by their very nature permeable, and there must be something that could be introduced. Nothing as ostentatious as the amputation and reattachment of a limb, but *something*.

Private View

A limestone cliff-face rises from a deep gorge, somewhere in the Pyrenees perhaps: sheer and impossible, yet cut with the stairways and cave-mouths of the anchorites, where no one has set foot for a thousand years.

Far below, deep in the ravine, a pattern of thaw: the white no longer white, where the snow has thinned, revealing scattered rocks and juniper bushes, scuffed tracks where something has been dragged back from the hunt.

I lower the lens, sit back on my heels and look again. With the naked eye, it's just pale lichen mottling the granite of an old headstone.

Disappointingly, I don't know its name. I started out with good intentions, meaning to learn about lichens so that I could recognise species, differentiate them one from another. I wanted to be able to stand in the quiet graveyard and speak their names, not least because their names are so exquisite. Where the Latin is meticulous, almost liturgical, the English is richly descriptive: woodscript, peppered moon, false map, gnome fingers, thrushwort, slender monk's-hood, rock tripe, streamside stippleback, lipstick powderhorn, speckled sea-storm, spiny rockshag, devil's matchstick, bloody comma.

I decided that the first step in this learning process was to look more closely. Some lichens are spectacular even at a glance: swags and flames and starbursts in vivid hues which prove that there is, contrary to the received wisdom, no colour too bright to exist in nature. Others are so subtle we don't notice them, just a shade or two lighter or darker than the substrate: a modest tinting, as if new paint has been tested cautiously for a match. Some are powdery and fissile, some are like sumptuous folds of cloth, others put forth buds which ripen into saucer-shaped fruits. But whatever form they take, it's impossible to see the detail without magnification. So I went and bought a hand-lens, and came back to start all over again: to explore this familiar churchyard as if it were new to me. Which it is. Each time I crouch close to a headstone and train my lens on its surface, I'm instantly relocated to a different world. A desert, criss-crossed with dusty roads. A patchwork of brown and golden forests. An old industrial zone with open chimneys, blasted and crumbling. A vast reef of silvery coral. A rocky outcrop bristling with giant fossils.

As I look, I'm reminded of the View-Master I had as a child: a stereoscopic toy, and a thing of amazement in those days before we owned a colour television. I was fascinated by the psychedelic effects you could get from something so ordinary-looking: a grey plastic box a bit like a camera, with two eyepieces, and a lever on the side which you pressed down with a finger to move the picture on. If you didn't press firmly enough the cardboard reel would only turn part of the way, and you would be stuck, stranded halfway between two slides. I had a dozen or so reels – I remember 'Man on the Moon', and 'Snow White and the Seven Dwarves' – but my favourite was 'The Seven Wonders of the World'. Looking at lichens through a hand-lens is a similarly three-dimensional, technicolour experience, a high-definition private view of somewhere about as remote from the monochrome and drizzle of the churchyard as the Hanging Gardens of Babylon from our 1960s cul-de-sac.

So I have been distracted from the effort of knowing, seduced by the pleasure of looking. I got as far as distinguishing crustose from fruticose from foliose, before pausing to notice how compelling they are: this one like candlewax thrown across a table by a draught, this one like spilt engine oil on a garage forecourt. I stared for ages at a woolly, mottled growth which reminded me of a heap of old fleeces I once saw in the Hebrides, thrown over the low wall of a disused sheepfold and left to rot there, harbouring their cultures of moss and insect life.

I did learn that a lichen is a double-act: alga and fungus, the two organisms living in symbiosis. And I discovered that they grow everywhere, not only on these ancient stones, but also on the churchyard trees, the brick wall, the metal bench, and the asbestos roof of the toolshed. A coat of green fur on a length of string dangling from a rowan branch. A curl of pencil shaving on a bright green pad of moss. Anywhere not too shaded and not too smooth will do; they need sunlight for photosynthesis, and a textured surface where they can take hold.

For those who really know and study lichen, churchyards are key sites, because they contain numerous separate micro-habitats, each made of different materials and exposed to different degrees of warmth, light and moisture. Multiple species can find sanctuary here, safe from human interference like chemical spraying and excessive tidiness, and some do not occur in any other environment but the churchyard. Certain specimens are nearly as old as the time-worn memorials they have colonised; they can become so sturdily established on the old stone that they continue to survive in spite of deteriorating air quality. Of those which have a special association with burial places, there is even one – *Parmelia saxatilis* – which bears the folk-name 'skull lichen'. This species grows on human bones, and at one time was highly prized for its medicinal properties, particularly if it was found on the skull of a hanged man. (That it was practical to harvest it at all implies a less fastidious attitude than ours towards decaying corpses.)

I will learn their names, I promise myself as I move from grave to grave, kneeling to inspect each stone in turn. I have begun to appreciate how lichenology can turn into an obsession. There are so many species, and the work of identifying and naming them is still going on. Who discovered, I wonder, through painstaking observation and comparison, that 'elegant centipede' (*Heterodermia leucomela*) was minutely distinct from 'powdered centipede'

(*Heterodermia speciosa*), or bearded jellyskin (*Leptogium saturninum*) from Lilliput jellyskin (*Leptogium tenuissimum*)? Such forensic attention to detail. Yes, I *will* learn.

I stop at the next stone, which bears a sprawling blue-white form, spotted with orange. I lean closer to examine it through the lens, and it springs to life, now resembling one of those satellite images of secretive states, with here and there the installations, the perfectly circular towers of unknown purpose, read as proof of illicit activity on the remote plains and steppes. They are enclosed in a kind of compound, defined by a thick black wall which has been breached on one side. What can that breach mean, I wonder. Has the compound been abandoned, or are its operations expanding? If I want to answer that question, I'll need to keep coming back and looking again.

Desires

Everyone knows the graveyard fears, but we rarely speak of its nexus of forbidden desires.

The wanton desire to go there after dark, and to test yourself against it, possibly to destruction, like the young couple we see in the horror film *La rose de fer*, who enter the cemetery on an impulse, all insouciance in spite of the gathering dark.

The primal desire to lie with a lover on a flat tomb, to seize life from the teeth of death, to claim your pleasure while you can. *The grave's a fine and private place, / But none, I think, do there embrace.*

Or to wait until you are alone, and to throw yourself prostrate on the graves. To get as close as possible to those who lie there, to press your whole body to the six feet of earth that separate you from them, and to know for sure that you are on the right side of it.

VII

The graveyard in summer. Ruts in the path, brim-
ming with gold. One blackbird setting a theme for
others to plagiarise. Horse chestnuts turning
their liver-spotted hands as they try to remember.

Bright and Sad

'Nothing then prevents a man both knowing and being mistaken about the same thing.'

Aristotle, *Prior Analytics*

I have seen the dead here. Not their ghosts – they have always managed to stay out of my sight, somehow, though there are days when I half expect to turn the corner behind the church and see a figure in the distance, under the yew, or by the field hedge where the churchyard gives way to open countryside. The monuments are sparser there, and the streets of the dead are softened and blurred. If I were to experience an apparition, that's where it would be, standing beside the stile and looking at the public footpath sign. Not translucent, not robed in white, nothing like that. I just imagine a kind of hesitancy about that figure, something equivocal in the way it stands and moves that will give it away. An impression that it doesn't quite belong in the here and now. A sense that whoever or whatever this figure is, it has slipped through a fault in the fabric somehow, and is as surprised to find itself here as I am to see it.

There's no one waiting under the yew or by the stile this afternoon. And it wasn't ghosts I saw all those years ago, but mortal remains. It happened on a Saturday in the summer of 1975. It was the morning after a colossal thunderstorm that had brought down power lines and washed loose slates from cottage roofs. I remember I had been sleeping with the window wide open – the heat had been intense those past two days – and I was jolted awake in the early hours by the lightning slashing my dream in two, and then the din of rain, sudden and total. Instead of getting up to close the window, I lay in bed as if possessed, and let the night tear itself to bits. Half a mile away, in the churchyard, the storm precipitated a sequence of events in the oldest section, close to the war memorial and the south door of the church. Rainwater hammered the dry earth, pooled on the surface, then coursed against a retaining wall. For a few minutes the wall resisted, but the bonds between its stones were weak with age, and as the deluge continued its footings shifted and loosened. There must have been a moment, as I lay there listening to the rain, when it reached a point of no return and part of the wall gave way and crashed onto the path. A few of the ancient graves collapsed and slid down the slope, their contents tumbling out after it.

No one would have heard it happen. I came this way the next morning, on the kind of beatific day which often seems to follow a storm like that: the air warm and still, puddles full of blue and gold. I remember approaching and seeing the mess of stone and earth and tree roots ahead of me. The bones and the roots were almost indistinguishable for a moment: both nakedly, almost luminously pale against the dark path. The ground had turned itself inside out in the storm, and what had been safely put away and hidden was spilled out into the light. I stepped cautiously over and around it, shocked and fascinated. Later that day, or so I heard, the vicar came running out of the vestry, cassock flapping, to remonstrate with some Sunday School kids who were japing around with a skull. Yesterday I stopped and examined that stretch of wall, and although more than forty years had passed I thought I could see the place where it was breached that night and then repaired, where the mortar was newer and pinker. For a moment, the past was so real and so close I could touch it with my fingertips.

Even before I looked at the churchyard wall and recalled the incident with the bones, I had been feeling rather ghostly myself, having slipped through the fabric between then and now and found myself not quite belonging in either. I had spent much of the day walking around the village, which was once *my* village, uncomfortably aware that I was a visitor from the past. When I arrived, I parked the car on the site of the old mill and walked down to the river. The mill fleam, originally a rushing course which turned the wheels and drove the machinery, silted up long ago. In this dry summer it was little more than a muddy ditch, idling silently under dense, overhanging willow and elder, the old sluices grown over with nettles and Himalayan balsam, the water a sullen glint beneath. I followed it to the place where it meets the River Dove, and the two run parallel for a stretch, separated by a walled embankment built in the nineteenth century to improve the outflow from the mill. Between the fleam and the river is a narrow wedge of land known as Dougie's Island. It's an overgrown and secluded place, fondly remembered by generations of children who would wade across, or swing over on a rope slung from the branch of a giant horse chestnut, to smoke and fish and play their wild games there. There was a game which involved swinging out on the rope, then launching just at the top of the curve so that you dropped and hung upside-down by your legs, and thrusting a pocket knife into the ground as far away as you could reach. Then it would be your friend's turn to swing out in the same way, snatch up the knife and sink it in a different spot. Hours could pass like this. But when I tried to visit Dougie's Island yesterday I found it gated and padlocked, and there was a *Keep Out* sign. I scanned the high trees for a frayed scrap of rope, but saw nothing.

I walked on through the village, thinking about the places we lived in as children, and how they are not just places in the way that everywhere else is a place. They are laid down in our bones as we grow. They are carried through life, vivid and textured and multi-dimensional. Time passes and experiences change us, but those places of childhood remain essential and immutable. Returning from exile many years later, we expect, despite the passage of time, to recognise the shallow depressions in the tarmac on the street corner where we used to play marbles, or to see the same faded display of birthday cards in the Post Office window. So I went from one old haunt to another yesterday, hoping to open a door into my childhood. I tried all the usual keys, but it seemed I'd been away too long and the locks had been changed.

We came to live in this village when I was eleven, and I spent my adolescence here. It was not far from our old home, but I recall the feeling of dislocation when we arrived, and how delicious that feeling was to me. We moved in the summer holidays, and those early weeks when I didn't know the place were rich with opportunities to explore, to get lost, to make my own discoveries. This had once been a thriving town with a lively history of battles, sieges and political intrigue. It was a quiet and obscure little place now, but there were still vestiges of the things which at various times in the past had lent it military and economic importance: a ruined fourteenth-century castle, and the remains of a glassmaking industry.

Before I arrived here yesterday, I already knew that the last of the old glassworks had gone, but all the same I was shocked to see for myself. A block of new maisonettes stood on the site of the factory, where boys I knew from school were apprenticed, trained to cut crystal with a diamond wheel. (I see at least one of those beautiful boys lies in the churchyard now.) Gone too was the half door where you used to be able to pause and watch a man draw out molten glass from a furnace, turn it and fold it like honey on the end of a pipe, and blow it into the shape of a vase or a goblet. Glassmaking was hot and thirsty work, and this village of a couple of thousand souls once had seventeen pubs. All but a few have gone, leaving only the taste of their names on the tongue: the Shoulder of Mutton, the Woolpack, the Hope and Anchor. They have melted away as if they were never there; with their curtained bay windows and ordinary front doors they are indistinguishable from the terraced houses that surround them.

Even the castle, surely the most solid and enduring of features, was not as I remembered it. This churchyard was my regular short-cut from home to the castle; I expect that's where I was going on the morning after the storm: to meet friends and scramble across the dry moat, scale the curtain wall and roam about inside. We were not supposed to be there, of course, but there was hardly ever anyone there to shoot us with arrows or pour boiling oil from the battlements, or even to shout at us and tell us to clear off. So we often had the run of the place. We felt it belonged to us, and would do it no harm. We ran up the dark spiral steps of the tower for the view from the top and the thrill of vertigo. There was a gap in the stonework known as Robin Hood's Leap, and there were boys a little older than me who claimed they had jumped across, but it must have been four feet wide with a terrifying drop beneath and I never saw anyone try. We chased each other along the ancient walls, over and around the site of the 'apartment' where Mary, Queen of Scots, was once imprisoned and wrote letters complaining about the smell of the privy. We read the old graffiti, put our fingers into the carved initials of those who had explored the place two centuries before us. But when I went to the castle yesterday I found it fortified against me, with gates and CCTV and a ticket booth (shut). There was a signboard advertising a wedding fayre and a medieval re-enactment.

Still, I reminded myself, I wasn't really here to see the castle or the glassworks. The true object of my visit was the churchyard, and a particular gravestone which told a story I had known since childhood. But this wasn't straightforward either. I couldn't find the right stone, though I was sure I knew where to look. I was alone among the graves, and there were so many of them. It was a wet day, and I had the wrong clothes for the weather.

After a damp, dispiriting search I decided to walk down to the old charity house, a small museum, and see whether someone there could help. As I arrived, the curator was closing up. When I mentioned the drowned boy, he said oh yes, and gave me startlingly precise directions: turn right at the top of the church path, past the war memorial, and it's the second of two flat tombs on the right. He glanced at his watch. Half-past six is the time to be there – you'll get the evening light on it then and you should be able to read the inscription.

He seemed too good to be true, but he looked too sure to be a ghost so I gave him the benefit of the doubt. I walked back in the rain, and found the tomb easily now, though troublingly it was not at all familiar. The stone looked too old and dark, it was mottled with moss and lichen and the lettering was too worn to read. The church clock said half-past six, but the light was dismal. I straightened and rubbed my back and considered giving up and going home. I glanced again towards the far boundary and the stile, wondering with a thump of the heart whether I had after all seen a figure at the edge of my vision. But there was no one there, just a kestrel hovering low near the hawthorn hedge. I stood and watched it hanging on its thread of air, tail spread for balance, wingtips extended like the fingers of a dancer. It fell hard on the long grass between graves, and rose, turning powerfully towards the trees, with something dangling from its claws – I couldn't see whether it was a vole or a field mouse or something else. Then the sun broke through, and I was too dazzled to go on looking. I turned back to the tomb, and saw that a few faint words had been drawn to the surface. It was miraculous, the way the light exposed them against the wet stone, like spilt bones against the path. *William ... Son who drowned ... River Dove ... Bathing.*

The story of the drowning had haunted me since childhood. I knew of it first not from the churchyard but from the church interior, where there was an unusual memorial, intricately carved from a piece of bog oak: a black lectern, with the details engraved on its brass plaque. I wanted to go in and see it again now, and to check the name, because William didn't seem right to me. I turned back along the path and tried the handle, but it was a day of locked doors.

*

Private Property, Keep Out read the sign at Dougie's Island. There was more, but it was plastered over with mud. The gate was slung with a heavy chain and padlock, double-locked with rust. I scrambled down the bank and under the bridge to try and get closer. Traffic grumbled overhead and reverberated in the dank and sepulchral space of the stone arches. I skidded down the slippery path and picked my way over gravel at the water's edge. I could hear birdsong on the island. There could be monkeys in there for all I knew. It was so densely overgrown the interior was completely screened from view. That, I remembered, had always been one of its attractions.

Another was its proximity to buried treasure. A few yards from where I was standing was the place where in 1831 a gang of workmen, digging out gravel from the riverbank to build the embankment, uncovered the first of a massive hoard of medieval silver. In all, 360,000 coins, caked and welded together with mud and bits of broken barrel, were quarried from this riverbank, where they had lain hidden since 1322. They had been the property of Thomas, Earl of Lancaster, the leader of a rebellion against Edward II. When the king and his army arrived to confront him he left the castle and fled northwards, leaving behind his war-chest, and somehow – whether by accident or design – the coins ended up buried in the gravel at the edge of the riverbed. Thomas was captured and beheaded and the treasure was never reclaimed. The king held an inquiry into its whereabouts, but the locals either didn't know or weren't saying.

Rumour drifted into legend, and legend into obscurity. For 500 years the river ran over the hiding place, day and night, and the hoard stayed secret and undisturbed, tucked in under the bank. Crowfoot, dropwort and milfoil sheltered it. The river ran fast and brown with meltwater in winter, steady and ticking with dragonflies in summer. Salmon, trout, dace and roach swam close, and herons stalked the gravel and watched for them. Willow and alder grew on the banks. The villagers milled their corn, cured sheepskins, cut withies to make baskets. The castle was demolished, rebuilt, demolished again. That bit of the past lay dormant, until the first of those nineteenth-century labourers stuck his shovel into the bank and heard the unforgettable clink of the blade against silver.

Then suddenly that stretch of river was swarming with men. They waded in and stood chest-deep in the water, digging with whatever tools they could find, riddling the stones and silt. Fistfights broke out as they vied for the best places and argued over ownership of the spoils. Dealers crowded the bridge and the riverbank, and silversmiths outbid each other to offer the best price. There were wild claims, protests, recriminations which lasted long after the gold rush was over. Twenty years later, a quantity of the treasure was cited as a motive in a case of double murder.

Where did all those precious coins go? A few are held in museums. Some were melted down. It's said that others are hidden in the village houses, some in a tobacco tin at the back of a cupboard, others forgotten in a box in the attic, but once again the locals are saying nothing. The river keeps its silence too. There are thought to be more still buried here, very close to where I was standing on my little gravel peninsula. Under the law of treasure trove they belong to the Crown, and it's been illegal to search for them since 1831, when the excavations were filled in on the orders of William IV. Nevertheless, during my teenage years there was the occasional rumour that someone's brother's best friend had gone out at night with a metal detector and come home with a pocketful of silver.

The river holds other secrets too. On a bitter February afternoon in 1936, a police sergeant and five or six men were assembled on the bank not far from that same spot. A grappling hook, thrown out on a length of rope again and again in the search for a child's body, snagged and caught its grasp on something. The rope tautened. There was a flare of excitement among the search party, though there had been false alarms already and no one wanted to get their hopes up. They had been dragging the river every day for nearly a month. It was difficult to know where to concentrate their efforts; as the sergeant knew from experience, when a river is swollen the racing surface water can carry a person a long way in a short time, but once drowning is complete the body sinks quickly to the bottom where there is almost no current at all. It meant they had a long stretch of river to work on, and it was painfully slow. Villagers had been taking turns to help in the search. A water-diviner who claimed to have a gift for finding lost things had volunteered her services, and the sergeant had swallowed his scepticism and lent her a boat. A crowd had gathered on the bank to watch as she was rowed downriver, holding a galvanised wire divining-rod and a glove belonging to the dead boy. But the days passed, and the weeks, and not a sign.

Sure enough, it was soon obvious that this object was far too solid and heavy to be a child. It was hauled out onto the bank, where it lay massive and enigmatic, like the corpse of some fabulous beast long thought extinct. It was the trunk of a prehistoric oak tree, which had been in the river for thousands of years. It had fallen – perhaps in a storm very like the one I heard on that summer night in 1975 – and lay where it fell, trapped in the riverbed, beginning the long process of becoming fossil. One of the search party, the father of the drowned boy, knelt and examined it: waterlogged, preserved by river mud, hardened by time and blackened by a reaction between the tannins in the wood and the iron in the subsoil. He was an inventor, who specialised in devising and constructing new machines for agriculture, so he knew about materials. He knew that bog oak was highly prized for furniture-making and ornamental work, and that this was quite a find. It was a piece of river-treasure, he decided, a gift in return for the lost child.

I was looking at the wrong grave, the wrong drowning. There have been so many drownings.

Today I've brought the curator with me – the one who predicted with such eerie accuracy the best time to read the worn inscription. His name is Robert, and I reckon that if anyone can unlock this place for me, it's him – he is the amanuensis of the churchyard, having taken on the task a couple of years ago of transcribing all the legible inscriptions, and drawn a map showing the locations of the stones. He'd be the first to admit that the map is not complete. There's a large wild area near the eastern boundary where a number of burials have themselves been buried, lost in the long grass. Dock, ground elder, plantain and wild carrot. Flat thistles studded with water droplets, like giant emerald spider webs. I was snared by brambles over there just a moment ago when I inadvertently put my foot through a deep hole, and hurt my ankle as I wrenched it out in a hurry, fearing I'd broken through into a grave beneath. But the long task of reclamation is underway, and today a group of volunteers from the local prison are here on a supervised placement, hard at work with strimmers, gradually bringing order out of the chaos. Old stone kerb-sets are emerging from obscurity for the first time in years, and the surface is bumped and ridged with the shapes of others yet to be found. It's a kind of archaeology. On our way along the strip of mown-grass path, we pause to look at a plot marked by a small oblong of green glass chips, as anonymous as a suburban lawn. An aged bouquet of artificial roses, bleached almost colourless but still stuck in a marble urn. A cherub with its head missing (It'll be around here somewhere, says Robert, rummaging in the long grass).

This morning I was waiting outside the charity house when Robert arrived, whistling and jangling a bunch of old keys. The minute I mentioned the bog-oak lectern, he understood straight away. He dashed inside to fetch something, then locked up again and led me here, past the church door, the village stocks and the war memorial, past the flat tomb of *William, Son who Drowned*, to this red marble headstone. It's decorated with an unusual carved pattern of climbing roses. I trace the pattern with my fingers, and feel the whole stone move, dangerously loose in its socket. Robert holds it steady with one hand as he brushes away the grass spat out by the strimmer so that I can read the inscription:

IN LOVING MEMORY OF
LEONARD,
THE BELOVED SON OF
CHARLES AND LILY GOODALL,
AGED 7 YEARS,
WHO WHILE RESCUING HIS COMPANION
LOST HIS OWN LIFE IN THE
RIVER DOVE AT TUTBURY ON JAN 28, 1936.

'GOD WILL SURELY ASK ERE I ENTER HEAVEN,
HAVE I DONE THE TASK WHICH TO ME WAS GIVEN.'

This story touched me deeply when I first heard it, I tell him. I remember thinking how extraordinary it was that this boy – younger than I was, the same age as my little brother – died rescuing another child. The gravestone rocks precariously on its roots as Robert lets go and fishes in his coat pocket to pull out a faded newspaper cutting he's brought from the archives to show me. It's a report on a ceremony which took place in the parish room back in June 1936, five months after the accident. The purpose of the occasion was the presentation of a posthumous award from the Royal Humane Society, in recognition of Leonard Goodall's courageous action. The coroner presented the citation to Leonard's twin brother, and made a speech in which he described the rescue as 'an example to small boys of the district as to what to do when a crisis arose'. I'm not sure how keen they would have been to follow it, says Robert dryly, given the outcome. The vicar then gave an address, saying that the occasion brought back 'memories bright and sad', and that 'the unselfish bravery shown would always be a light in that town of Tutbury'. In such an act of self-sacrifice, he said, Leonard was 'one with the noblest and best of our race'.

Leonard's is not the only drowning among the dead of this place; the Dove has claimed many lives. It's an unpredictable river, quick to change its mood. Even in the most benign weather it can still be swollen and heady with the rain that fell two or three days ago, running much deeper and faster than it looks. In conditions like that, it's a fierce journey from the source on Axe Edge, high in the gritstone hills of the Dark Peak, down through limestone gorges, ash woods and open farmland to the Trent. In its wilder tempers it snatches things from its banks – trees, fence-posts, fishermen's gear – and sweeps them down with it. It scores the ancient boundary between Staffordshire and Derbyshire, but it makes no discrimination, breaking its banks and overflowing into both its counties equally. In the eighteenth century it was rather fancifully styled 'the British Nile', thanks in part to its habit of flooding suddenly and dramatically – as one historian noted, 'nearly inundating the whole valley, and carrying off sheep, and sometimes cattle, before any danger is suspected'.

People, too – swimmers, fishermen, walkers, workers – have sometimes been carried off like this. Others have gone of their own accord, pockets loaded with stones. But the highest death-toll is among children, who are caught out as they play in or near the water. Many of these accidents happen at the weir that lies on a broad bend in the river, in open fields, right under the eye of the castle, which has seen it all before. In the middle of a dry summer the water slips obediently over, sparkling in the sunshine, and at the weekend there are often kids larking about there, taking turns to slide down the fish-pass, slippery with moss and riverweed. But when the river is running high, it's all too easy to misjudge it, crash onto the rocks in the race below and be swept away on the current.

In winter the dangers are different, though the outcome is the same. Standing by the red marble stone, Robert and I share what we know, piecing together the story of what happened to Leonard Goodall. January 1936 saw severe weather across the Midlands, with ice and heavy snow. Overnight on 27th there was a rapid thaw. The next morning Leonard went to call for his friend Douglas, who lived with his grandparents at a neighbouring farm, and they decided to walk down and see the river. The flooding was so extensive that the fields around it were one brilliant sheet of water. It was irresistible. The boys waded in. They were very familiar with the fields and the river, and they thought they knew where the bank was, but as they approached the weir Douglas walked into a deep hole and was immediately out of his depth, drowning in fast water. He was snatched under and along and had to fight his way back to the surface. 'When I came up, I found Leonard by my side,' he said at the inquest. 'He was struggling, and caught hold of my arm, but I pushed it off and caught hold of his hand, but the current wrenched him loose.' At that moment, Douglas's feet touched the bank and he was able to haul himself to safety. It was all over in a few seconds. When he looked back, he saw Leonard swept along and tumbling over and over in the current. He chased along the bank, but soon lost sight of him.

When I first discovered Leonard's story, it seemed to me to belong no less to 'history' than the tale of Mary, Queen of Scots imprisoned in the castle, or the Earl of Lancaster executed for treason. I didn't have much sense of chronology then; the past was the past.

The story has lived with me and in me ever since, like Robin Hood's Leap and the game with the rope-swing. But as I've grown and changed through life experience, my perspective on it has shifted. To begin with I saw it all through Leonard's eyes, then a little later through the eyes of the friend whose life he saved, but in adulthood I'm prone to imagining the terrible grief of the parents.

Still, throughout the years they have all been characters in a story: figures from the past, long before I was born, rather than individuals with lives as intense as my own. But now I've made the electrifying discovery that one of them is still alive.

The accident at the weir ended Leonard's life, but for the other boy, the rescued one, it was an event lived through and beyond. I have always wanted to know more about that boy, the survivor. No one I spoke to in the village seemed to know what had happened to him. It was all such a very long time ago, and those few who remembered knew only the basics: a drowned child, an act of heroism. The other boy was probably dead by now, I supposed, but I wondered what kind of life he had led and how that early experience had affected him in adulthood. There was very little to go on. The red gravestone did not name him, but the story it told could not exist without him. He was an eloquent silence. His absence was a kind of presence.

I found him, eventually, by guesswork, tip-off and lucky accident. In time I had not only his name, but an address where I could write to him. I hesitated. If he was still alive, he'd be ninety-two. He might be very frail, or have lost his memory. He might not want to be reminded of painful events from long ago. But my careful letter was answered immediately with a phone call from John, his friend and carer. Yes, Doug would be glad of the chance to tell me about what happened that day. It was something he hadn't talked about for many years, and he knew it might be his last chance. His memory was terrible, John warned me, so come in the afternoon: afternoons were not as bad as mornings.

I have driven out into the Dark Peak to meet him, in a small gritstone village not very far from the source of the Dove. A glance at the map showed Doug's cottage obscurely located at the end of a narrow and indiscernible lane, and it turns into one of those journeys where the satnav gets into a closed loop, insisting again and again that you make a U-turn where possible. I could spend the rest of the afternoon at the wheel, circumnavigating the village square, rolling again and again past its small series of attractions: café, doctor's surgery, war memorial. I'm no less disorientated than I was when I stumbled about in the churchyard, searching for Leonard's grave in all the wrong places. In the end I abandon the car in a side road, and wander on foot through the afternoon rain, until I see the lit oblong of an open doorway, and John waiting to greet me.

Doug is very pleased to meet someone who knew his old village: the pubs, the glassworks, the castle. He once excavated the ancient well at the castle; he brings out a photograph which shows him roped up and about to be belayed down in front of a small audience of puzzled children. I ask him what he found down there and he gives a short laugh: nothing. With a little encouragement, he reminisces about the hoard of coins, and an occasion when he went down to the riverbank with his granddad's coal shovel and tried his luck, in spite of the prohibition. We swap stories about the old mill, the fleam, Dougie's Island. He grins and says he's always wondered whether his parents named him Douglas because they were on the island when ... you know.

He sits attentively in an armchair wedged into a narrow space between bookshelves, pale-eyed, long white hair to his shoulders, waiting for me to ask about the day of the drowning. I take a deep breath, and ask.

It had rained a lot, he tells me, in a simple, matter-of-fact voice, and it was hard to see where the edges were. There were inlets in the field, and we both fell in.

There's a flicker of silence, and he's back in that long-ago moment, reliving it. He's forgotten I'm there. He's looking not at me, nor at the desk behind me heaped with books and papers and empty mugs, nor the wet square of the window above it. It's as if he can see through a different kind of window, a square cut in the gyre of dusty air above the fan heater. He's staring directly through it onto that January morning in 1936.

I was *here*, he says, touching the arm of his chair – and he was *there*, lifting his thin old hand and pointing tremulously somewhere over my shoulder. He was out in the middle – I could see him – but I was at the side – and I felt the bank with my foot – and I climbed out. Then I ran home – I swam across the fleam and ran home.

The moment passes. The only sound is the rattle of the fan heater. John brings tea and Doug sits in silence for a minute or two. His eyes are watery. I can't tell whether remembering is painful for him, or whether it's just the vagueness of old age, the effort of catching the thread and losing it again.

I bring out a copy of the newspaper report about Leonard trying to save his life, and the presentation of the Royal Humane Society award. I unfold it and start to read it out. I'm expecting him to be pleased to hear the story again after all this time, perhaps gratified that it hasn't been entirely forgotten. It's a shame his eyes are not good, because look, there's a photograph, the coroner presenting the vellum certificate to a small blurred figure which must be Leonard's twin brother.

But he interrupts me and pushes the paper away. No, no, he says vehemently, that's not what happened.

I'm not sure what he means. Perhaps he's getting tired. I exchange a glance with John, who shrugs.

I fold the newspaper cutting, thinking it might be time to leave. But then Doug speaks up again. It wasn't like that at all. It wasn't true. They said it was, but it wasn't.

I sit in stunned silence a moment. *It wasn't true?*

It was an ordinary accident, he says. He just fell in. We both fell in, but he was much smaller than me. I told them, but they wouldn't listen, they made up their own story.

The folded paper twitches in my hand, as if it's alive.

It must have been a comfort to Leonard's parents, I say in the end.

Yes, he nods. Yes. Well, they were the ones who said it. It was their idea.

The house fills up with silence. I glance carefully around the tiny living room, which doubles up as a library, crammed floor to ceiling with books on geology, archaeology and local history. Stacked above and between are giant cardboard tubes holding handmade maps and drawings of caves and lead-mines and underground tunnels. On the wall is a grainy black-and-white photograph of Doug as a young man, standing grinning by a pothole, holding an improvised raft made of inner tubes. The whole of his working life was spent navigating underground worlds, assessing their size and safety and viability for mining and quarrying. He made a specialism of exploring and mapping flooded shafts and chambers, wading and diving his way through deep water in enclosed spaces. It was dangerous work, and he had several narrow escapes. It strikes me that this cannot be a coincidence, so I ask him how it affected him, the accident. He shakes his head and says no, it didn't affect him, he just forgot about it and got on with his life.

But when I've drunk my tea and thanked him and am standing at the door, he calls after me, saying again: *I was there, but they wouldn't listen to me.*

I drive back in the rain, with the wipers keening. I think of weather and water, dust and shadow. The boy who nearly drowned, and the man he became. The life he made for himself, searching the dark spaces underwater, mapping them and making them safe. I think of the red marble headstone, inscribed with an unequivocal message of heroism, but unstable and leaning.

I cast my mind back to the coroner's report. First the coroner, and then the police sergeant on duty on the day of the drowning, take turns to question Doug. They are understandably keen to get answers, to arrive at a story which holds together. He is not forthcoming. They become insistent, and it starts to sound like a cross-examination. They put it to him that Leonard's position in the middle of the river and the fact that he caught hold of his arm suggests that he had jumped in to rescue him. Doug says nothing. They ask again. Again he says nothing. Can he think of any other explanation? Well then, doesn't he agree that this is what happened? Doesn't he agree that Leonard was saving his life?

Perhaps he wasn't sure he could trust his own memory, or perhaps he simply felt the pressure of other people's wishes and couldn't resist. They were the adults, after all. The little boy's parents were distraught. The whole town was gripped by the story. He knew what people were saying: that he was old enough to know better, should never have gone to the river that day, should himself have shown some heroism. What boy of twelve has to be rescued by a seven-year-old? And who would want to hear that this was just a pointless accident, 'misadventure', nothing but sudden, random loss? Who wouldn't welcome any glimmer of redemption, anything to mitigate the sorrow, anything to make some sense of it all?

Yes, he must have done, he says at last.

By the time I get back to Tutbury, the sky has cleared and the churchyard has an almost festive appearance, the grass and the floral tributes glittering in the sun. In the newer section, there's a grave decorated with a red model tractor and trailer. Another is adorned with a line of cherubs, fairies, butterflies and a smiling elephant, one behind the other as if forming an orderly queue for the afterlife. Plot No. 8, though, is occupied only by a slab on the grass bearing a single word: RESERVED.

'We ought not to take a short view of life,' said the vicar in his address. 'It is a matter outside our hands.' The hall was packed with clergymen, dignitaries, police officers, relatives, Girl Guides, schoolchildren and local people. But those events, which gripped the town and dominated the news headlines for weeks, are slipping out of living memory. The only witness to what happened at the river that day was a traumatised twelve-year-old boy. Now he found himself swept along on a different kind of current: a narrative he didn't believe in but couldn't control. At least that's how he sees it today, a lifetime later, his powers of memory slipping away, but still vividly recalling that painful dissonance between what he experienced and what was inscribed on vellum and presented in the parish room in front of half the town. He kept his silence. The account which endures is the one chiselled into red marble.

We can't know for sure. Because this story mattered to me as a child, it never occurred to me that it might not be definitive. But history is always a matter of interpretation. Even my own childhood is a story I tell myself.

I am accustomed to thinking of the graveyard as a kind of archive, a source of information which is not available elsewhere – either because it has been lost with the passage of time, or because it describes lives which have been considered too ordinary and unremarkable to be worth holding on to. We simply do not have the capacity to remember everything. In fact, we remember almost nothing. The small scrap of detail on a gravestone can make it possible to retrieve the individual. It can open up a story, spring a life into three dimensions. It can be the beginning of a long act of reconstruction, perhaps even of rescue. That's if the stone is right, the detail true. We speak of 'hard' facts, 'solid' information, and there are few things harder or more solid than stone. But someone tells the mason what words to put there. Someone sits and composes the message.

The view from here, out across the Dove valley, is just as ambiguous. The hazy shapes of distant hills. Fields, copses, the spire of a country church. The shapeless sprawl of the coffee factory, red and grey, with its two white chimneys. Between them the river, which has always meant so much to the people who lived and died here – fertility for the land, power for the machines, recreation, death by drowning, places to hide things and find things – but which cannot be reduced to those meanings or contained within any of their stories. It runs on regardless, as water must, from source to sea.

I leave the churchyard, taking the path by the mended wall, and walk where I have walked many times before, over the sunlit pastureland of Castle Hill and down to the weir. As I go, I imagine a different scene. A winter day, a great thaw. A sense of occasion: it's the day of the king's funeral, and there are black flags in the Post Office window. I see the two boys ahead of me: the taller one leading the way, the other smaller but determined to keep up, wading through the floods in their wellies, shouting and laughing and splashing. The fields they know so well are shining and scudding with clouds; the sheep have gathered on the higher ground, where the tussocky grass shows through, but closer to the river it's browner and more restless and you can see a row of fence-posts and a gate sticking up out of the water, which is quite exciting. The younger one is wishing his twin brother was here to see it, but enjoying the novelty of this small adventure with the grown-up boy from the farm, who is old enough to take the bus to school on his own and knows a lot about the world. The older one is happy cracking jokes and answering questions and showing how brave he is. Over a footbridge, over a stile, and I'm at the water's edge, thinking of both of them – the one who survived, and had to run back the way he'd come to break the news; and the one who didn't. I stand and stare into the water for a long time, dragging the river with my eyes, like someone looking for treasure. It's not a token of the past I'm looking for, like an ancient tree or a coin. Not the boy himself – I've never had any luck with ghosts. But a little silver key, perhaps, which will open the locked door between that moment and this, and let him back through.

Reaper

An old churchyard is the very place I might expect to see a tall figure with a scythe: the Grim Reaper, here on his eternal mission to bring in the human harvest, or to act as psychopomp, escorting the souls of the newly dead from this life to the next. I stand frozen with my hand on the gate, gripped by the power of that image, a staple of so many stories and pictures, passed down through the generations since medieval times. The distant figure is motionless too, the scythe raised. I have time then to notice that he is wearing not a hooded robe but jeans and a T-shirt. After a long, suspended moment I hear voices, and the spell breaks. The scythe is lowered, a second figure approaches from the other side of the church. Then a third.

Scything is re-establishing itself as a sustainable way of managing churchyards. The grass is not cropped short and uniform as it is with a mechanical mower; there's more variation and unevenness in the cut, which helps maintain a variety of habitats and encourages the survival of a wide range of species. Managed the old way, our burial places come to look less like suburban lawns and more like small nature reserves.

It's slower, too, and quieter and less invasive than other methods: the petrol mower, belching out fumes; the strimmer, that rackety piece of kit, chopping indiscriminately through everything it meets, spraying out grass and stones. Instead, there is the rhythmic swish of the blade, the chink-chink-chink of the sharpening tool, the occasional burst of laughter. The three figures move among the venerable old stones, each swinging the scythe in an arc, swivelling at waist and hip, shifting the weight from the right foot to the left with every stroke of the blade. There's a technique which has to be learned; it would once have been passed down from one generation to the next, men and women, and it would have been unusual in country places not to have some facility with the scythe. Now there are workshops and courses, enthusiasts, activists. Learning to scythe has become an enjoyable way to spend the weekend after too long sitting at a desk, and to contribute to community life by helping look after your local churchyard.

As an aeroplane labours overhead, the workers are cutting their broad swathes and the grass is piling up in windrows to dry. It may be picturesque, but of course it's hard work. To mow a field this size, powered only by your own muscle and blood and breath, is a thirsty and tiring endeavour. But like any repetitive activity – swimming, laying bricks, kneading dough – scything can become meditative. The movements, practised until they come right, can take you out of your habitual psychological space and into a kind of nirvana. In *Anna Karenina*, Tolstoy has Levin experience something like this; the longer he works, the more frequently he feels 'moments of unconsciousness in which it seemed not his hands that swung the scythe, but the scythe mowing of itself, a body full of life and consciousness of its own, and as though by magic, without thinking of it, the work turned out regular and well-finished of itself'.

I have not personally experienced this form of bliss. My own experiments in scything are limited to a single attempt, twenty-odd years ago, to cut an overgrown suburban garden. We had utopian visions for that garden: wildlife pond, miniature orchard, woodland-edge habitat. The only part we realised was a tiny wildflower meadow, which proved surprisingly easy to establish and flickered with bees and butterflies all through the early summer. In July, when the flowers had set seed, it was cut down. Only once did I try my hand with the scythe. Without adjusting the haft and lay of the blade, and with no instruction or practice, I made slow and damaging progress, hacking rather than slicing through the stems, digging the blade into the ground and chipping up chunks of soil and root. Watching these three and their elegant progress across the churchyard, I see how expert they are. The skilled mower sweeps with the scythe, the blade strokes the ground, the grass falls. Every ten minutes or so they stop to hone the blade. I watch one of them now as she flips the scythe to rest on its handle, holds it by the snath and runs the whetstone over the blade a few times to restore its bite. At some point in the afternoon, it will need peening, or cold-forging, the edge of the blade hammered out to make it thinner and keener.

Time honours and hallows these sounds: the rhythmic swinging of the scythe, the sigh of the grass as it falls, the work with stone and peening-jig. If the dead were to wake and hear them, they would settle back in their graves, reassured by familiarity. And the living, who come in from the street to sit in the shade of the old yew and watch, are reminded of the cycle of growth and harvest, steady and inescapable, though they thought they had broken faith with it long ago. They see once more that they too are part of that cycle, just as their ancestors were, and they are simultaneously soothed and chilled to the bone by the knowledge that some things, at least, continue in the old way.

Square 6

Gaps and absences are everywhere: in the writing of history, the telling of a story, the drawing of a family tree. Like dark matter, they make up most of the human cosmos. My own family is riddled with them, particularly on my father's side. Hardly anything is known about his ancestors. Until the last six months of his life, he could still be coaxed into talking about his grandparents, but his memory was going, and they had become elusive figures even to him.

Memory is the evidence I have that I am the same person I have always been. If I begin to doubt it for some reason, I can go in search of that evidence, returning to the towns I lived in long ago, hunting in their streets and parks for something I will recognise. If I can remember what happened to me back then, I can pull off the necessary trick. I can go on believing in the persistence of myself through time, of *me* as a coherent and discrete individual. My memories are the touchstones on which I assay my identity. Dementia confronts me with the terror of losing this continuity of self, of existing only from moment to moment.

Typically it's short-term memory which goes first. Dad took to phoning with the same question five or six times over a weekend. Which day was I coming to see him. What time was his hospital appointment. Where did he keep his cheque book. The questions spread, like shadow claiming more and more ground. Did he have a washing machine. Whose were all these tablets in the medicine cabinet. How could the paper say it was February when we hadn't had Christmas yet.

Earlier memories persisted, though it took an effort to retrieve them. Belatedly I started recording his voice as he talked about his childhood. He was still able to tell a story, though when I listen I notice how the narrative is punctuated by silences where he has forgotten a name or has to think about what comes next. Then he recovers and continues, and the story is still vividly told. I hear myself laughing when he talks about his father taking calves to market in the Austin 7, or a puritanical headmaster bursting into the school hall one lunchtime, snatching 'Sentimental Journey' from the record-player and dashing it to pieces on the floor. I'd heard these stories many times, but Dad still knew how to tell them.

Later his command of language would falter, and storytelling would move beyond his range. For the first time in his life, he found himself lost for words. Witnessing this process, slow but inexorable, I began to understand what it meant not only for my father but also for the fund of family history he held. We could search in the census records and parish registers, find out names, draw a map. But the names would lie inert on the page as they do on these old stones. My father was the last guardian of those family stories, and when he lost them we all lost them.

On my mother's side there's more to go on, but even so I had been living in London for several years before I realised how close I was to the house where she was born. I had begun sorting through her papers and regretting, in that way sons and daughters do, that I hadn't asked her more about her life while I had the chance. So I took the Central Line to Leyton, with the address on a scrap of paper in my pocket, and found the place. I stood on the pavement in a dreamlike state, half expecting to see the door swing open and my mother waiting there, six years old, holding her father's hand.

If my mother had been alive and here with me now, she would have been surprised to find her birthplace still standing and very little changed – one in a row of late-Victorian terraces, two-up, two-down – though she would have been scandalised by the prices these modest houses fetch today. It would have been so recognisable that the sight of it would have brought to mind long-forgotten details of the past. She would have found the surroundings oddly mixed: in some ways intensely familiar and in others drastically altered. These days, the street comes to an abrupt stop at one end, at a pallid and sprawling retail complex. But at the other end the entrance to Coronation Gardens has hardly changed, and inside are the same formal flowerbeds, bandstand and fountain she would have known from early childhood.

The survival of this street seems close to miraculous, since during the Second World War hardly a house in the neighbourhood escaped Blitz damage. My mother's family somehow managed to find the means to move out east to Gidea Park, where they were bombed nevertheless. It's almost unimaginable, the persistence of childhood through all that fire and shattering. I remember how she described watching her father, in the minutes after the blast, crawling blindly through broken glass and feeling around for his spectacles.

I can visit my mother's birthplace, and I was with her in her deathplace, but she doesn't have a grave I can visit. When she died, we had her body cremated and the ashes scattered. It's the modern way. Indeed, in my family it has been the way for generations. My ancestors on both sides were staunch Methodists, and therefore early adopters of cremation at a time when the Church of England was still resistant to the idea. For Methodists it presented no great difficulty, thanks to their unsentimental attitude towards the body – that 'tenement of clay' which temporarily houses the soul – and their belief in a resurrection which is unequivocally spiritual rather than corporeal. Perhaps it's due to this family inheritance that I am able to enjoy graveyards the way I do. They are not personal for me. The installation of a gravestone, the tending of a grave, are things I find interesting and touching, but they are not part of my own experience. The fire and the wind have taken my forebears for a hundred years and more, and will no doubt perform the same service for me when the time comes.

But that day in Leyton was a kind of pilgrimage, and I was attending the sites of my mother's early life: the house where my grandmother gave birth to her, the street where they walked to buy groceries, the park where she played with her brother. I was on a physical journey, visiting and reconstructing her embodied past. And as I stood there and thought about her beginnings, and cast the line deeper, further back to what came before, I knew I must find a family grave. There had to be one somewhere, I told myself.

Manor Park Cemetery in East London was laid out on land purchased from a neighbouring farm. The auction offered '300 acres of most superior and productive market garden land, some of which is singularly adapted for building'. But when the deal had been struck and the workmen came with their picks and shovels, their job was to dig down rather than build up, and the residents who settled here have never left.

There are hundreds of war graves, many of them the familiar Portland stones, identical in size and shape, manufactured and maintained by the Commonwealth War Graves Commission on the principle of equal treatment for all. But like most neighbourhoods, the cemetery is a mixture of grander and more ordinary addresses: many packed in tight like the terraces in my mother's street, but others smarter and more spacious. Near the cemetery gates, workmen are planting petunias in front of the white marble monument of Jack Cornwell, a 'First Class Boy' who was awarded the Victoria Cross after his death in the Battle of Jutland at the age of sixteen. Both world wars had a devastating impact on this part of London. During the Blitz neither the living nor the dead were spared; the cemetery was bombed and the chapel destroyed in an air raid.

But my purpose here goes back well before all that. I've come in search of Ethelind, my mother's paternal grandmother, who was buried at Manor Park in May 1902. She was twenty-eight, and had died of puerperal septicaemia. She had survived the ordeal of childbirth itself, but two days later she developed a fever. The infection got into her bloodstream, where it spread quickly and catastrophically, causing the circulation to shut down and the vital organs to fail one by one. Hers was not an unusual death; the days immediately after delivery were a time of danger and dread, right up until the 1940s and the age of antibiotics.

In my hunt for a family grave, Ethelind's seemed my best hope. But would I be able to find it on one of these cramped and crumbling streets? A search of the burial records provided me with a reference number: 379 in Square 6. Since this didn't tally with the cemetery plan at all, I made further inquiries, which revealed that Square 6 had been 'reclaimed' in the 1950s, and built up to be used for new burials. I learned also that number 379 was not unique to Ethelind. It was not an individual plot, but a 'public' or common grave. Eight people were buried there in that same week in 1902. No headstone or memorial was erected.

None of this should have surprised me. Ethelind's place of death was her home in Gurley Street, in a desperately poor and overcrowded part of the East End. It was blighted by unemployment, and those who were in work were mostly casual labourers with no steady or dependable income. Destitution was so close you could see it with your own eyes in the ominous form of the workhouse a couple of streets to the north. There can have been no question of purchasing a grave or installing a stone with her name on it, and no doubt that Methodist attitude towards the death of the body and the corporeal remains came in useful in making the hard reality easier to bear.

I have found my way to the corner of the cemetery, near the perimeter fence. The most desirable plots, for those who could afford them, were near the centre, close to the entrance gates and the chapel of rest; but it's greener and less oppressive out here on the edge, where the poor were laid in their common graves. There are big old trees here, survivors from the previous life of this land as fields and copses. A digger hums and clatters a few yards away, excavating a new grave. There are heaps of freshly dug earth covered in tarpaulins, and wooden boards for the workmen to walk on. These more recent graves reflect the richly multicultural character of East London, and it's a riot of colour in the spring sunshine. Huge floral tributes spell out names: OLUSEGUN, MOSZEK, HOI CHAN, EUNICE. Where there are headstones, they are mostly the ubiquitous polished black marble, but there's white too, and gold lettering, and gardens marked off with plastic fencing. There are memorials cut in the shapes of books and hearts, a grand piano, even a replica BMW on a granite plinth with a photograph of its late owner propped up in the driving seat.

I have located the place where Square 6 used to be, and with my plan of the old layout I am able to guess at the rough location of 379, though of course there is nothing on the ground to verify it. Now I stand approximately at the graveside of my great-grandmother, and of the seven others who shared this space with her. I feel suddenly self-conscious, wondering what kind of ritual, what words or gesture might be appropriate. Census records have allowed me to get a glimpse of the mixed constituency which makes up a common grave like this one. Along with Ethelind were buried two babies, two children, a forty-three-year-old gas stoker, the wife of a cabinet-maker, and a tailor with a violent criminal record. All died that same week in May, and all were buried at public expense in a pauper's grave. They were miscellaneous company. But the dead don't care about such things.

I count them off silently, naming all eight of them in turn. I think of kneeling and touching the ground, but I've seen the diggers working and I don't think this earth would know Ethelind any more. In any case, it's not the detail of what happened to her body that grieves me. When I was a child, my grandfather would occasionally speak of the loss of his mother. For him and his siblings, it was not only a bereavement but also a moment of dislocation and trauma in which their lives changed completely. Their father had been scraping a labourer's living, first on the construction of the Blackwall Tunnel and then as a platelayer on the railway; now he found himself alone with five children under the age of eight, including a newborn baby. He had no family in London, and no support to help him cope, so the children were sent to live with relatives 250 miles away in Middlesbrough, where they were separated and taken in by various aunts and uncles. Two of them died there – one from a seizure, one from a dog bite – and for those who survived things were never the same again.

Ethelind's second son was resilient, though. Twelve years later, he was back: Walter, my not-yet grandfather. He had just turned nineteen, and had landed a new job in London. These were the first days of war, which would throw the points of his life again very soon. But today he had taken the train to Leyton and was looking for lodgings. He walked past the gates of Coronation Gardens and along the same street where I walked last week. He didn't know the area or anyone who lived here, but he had been provided with a contact. In his jacket pocket he had a scrap of paper, very much like the one I held in my hand when I was there, and with the same address noted down on it. His cousin had written ahead, vouching for him as an honest, industrious, chapel-going young man. He stood on the pavement just where I stood, looking at the same front door, rehearsing what he would say. When he knocked, the door was opened by a young woman called Elsie. She had eyes the same colour as mine, and was wearing a blue velvet dress with a lace collar. It's an encounter which has passed into family legend.

I don't know whether he visited his mother's grave while he was in town; there was nothing for him to see, after all. If he did come, I hope the sun was blazing down on Square 6, the way it is today, burning off the squalor and the sorrow and dignifying the place with light. Either way, it was not the past that mattered now, but the moment on the doorstep: the moment when he and my not-yet grandmother saw one another for the first time, and the future began again.

VIII

Graveyard charms and tributes:
Battery operated candle
Happy Birthday balloon
Photograph of country cottage
Packet of Crawford's custard creams (150g, 85p)
Patchwork blanket (very wet)
Phone with moss growing in socket
Photograph of couple in Christmas hats
Dog's lead, carefully coiled
Old penny, squashed flat (under wheel of train?)
Broken mirror, full of sky
Running shoe, size 8
Painted stone in shape of heart
Photograph of child in pram
Flag of unknown nation (Congo? Guyana?)
Pink dolphin figurine
Silver butterfly on stick
Photograph of horse looking over gate
Rusty lighter (still works)
CD Rick Astley (*Never Gonna Give You Up*)

Dust

Some places become graveyards overnight. There is a defining event which turns a place suddenly from ordinary field or wood into mass grave. In some cases, this is not understood until many years afterwards, when the testimony of local people and the work of forensic archaeologists come together in an effort to reconstruct the story of an atrocity. In others, there can be no doubt; the defining event is a natural disaster like an earthquake or volcanic eruption, which transforms the landscape and buries the bodies of its victims beyond recovery.

When I was growing up, my friends and I would sometimes cycle along the lanes to the nearby village of Fauld, to run around and picnic in 'the crater'. This was a strange wooded valley, three-quarters of a mile wide, with sides that dropped away abruptly to a depth of about 400 feet. I suppose that we must have been told what had happened there, how it came to be the way it was, but that was ancient history as far as we were concerned. What mattered to us was that this was an eerie and exciting place to explore.

The crater was linked to another of our favourite haunts, the site of the old plaster mill. It was near Dougie's Island, close to where the hoard of medieval coins was unearthed. The mill was built during the cotton boom of the eighteenth century, and was later converted to crush and grind gypsum into plaster for the construction industry. It was demolished when I was very young, and I have no true memory of it, just second-hand impressions gained from the pictures I've seen and the stories I've heard over the years. The place where it stood was just rough ground when I knew it, a good place to play tag and lurky, and to discover a few relics of its industrial past here and there: bits of railway line, mysterious pieces of metal that might have been parts of pulleys or conveyor belts. The site has since been landscaped and made into a children's playground, and one of the original millstones lies propped up on the grass like a toppled statue, a reminder of the old regime.

Once the spinning jennies were gone, the mill began its second life. Week in, week out, for eighty years, huge blocks of gypsum were brought by narrow-gauge railway from the mines up the road at Fauld. The Stonepit Hills there are riddled with tunnels, galleries and shafts, the legacy of centuries of gypsum-working, first by quarrying and working outcrops, and later by deep mining. The hills yielded a good supply of alabaster, that glistening, translucent white rock, veined yellow and orange, that was so highly prized for statues, altarpieces and funerary monuments. But most of the extraction was ordinary soft gypsum, a mineral substance and a versatile material, ubiquitous on building sites as loose plaster, as blocks, as drywall, or mixed with anhydrite to make cement. Quarrying and processing it was a lucrative business hereabouts, and a major source of employment.

Photographs indicate the scale and complexity of the mill, showing a vast five-storey building with tall chimneys, a broad channel of water, ponds and dams, and yards and sheds for loading and storing the raw material and the manufactured products. It must have been one of the dustiest places on earth. Every beam, every stanchion, every rung and cable was thick with plaster dust.

Just before the outbreak of the Second World War, some of the gypsum tunnels were identified as a suitable place to store ammunition. Work began to requisition them and make them ready for their new and critical role. It was meant to be top secret, but the people who lived in the area knew all about it and called it 'the dump'. It was staffed by servicemen from a small RAF base nearby, and later they were joined by Italian prisoners of war.

To begin with, the dump was used only to store new ammunition ready for use when needed, but as the war progressed it was extended and took on a reception and maintenance role too. Jettisoned bombs were retrieved and returned here, often in a damaged or defective state, and still primed with their detonators, which had to be removed before the bombs were assigned to storage and repair. There was only one safe way to dismantle one of these bombs. It must be taken to an isolated cavern called the exploder bay, and the explosive chipped out using a copper chisel. It was imperative that only a chisel made of copper be used for this task, because other metals could raise a spark and detonate the bomb. These were the rules. But it was wartime; the workload was heavy, and increasing by the week, and manpower was short.

At 11.11 on 27 November 1944, there were two explosions. The first was like a warning shot, but fired too late, leaving no time for anyone to heed it. The second, ear-splitting blast was one of the largest non-nuclear explosions anywhere in the world. It was heard in London, 120 miles away, and the tremor showed up on seismographs in Geneva and Casablanca. The earth was ripped open, and thousands of tons of rocks and gypsum were flung into the air. 'There was a blinding flash,' said one eyewitness, 'and it looked like a great mountain in front of you. The stuff stood up so high – pieces as big as railway engines were going up in the sky.' A reservoir was smashed, sending an avalanche of mud and water over the dump and the surrounding countryside, drowning workers underground and civilians above. An entire farm, complete with farmer and wife, workers, animals, barns and machinery, was atomised, wiped from the map. In Tutbury, windows burst from their frames and chimneys collapsed. The plaster mill, along with its yards and ponds and sheds, was engulfed in a huge cloud of its own dust.

Today I returned to the crater, to see what the last forty years have done to it. I'd been warned that access is restricted nowadays: that you could still walk to the edge and get a view of it, but the site itself was fenced off and out of bounds to the public. Sure enough, it wasn't long before I was diverted from my old familiar route and lost my way. The woodland was so much thicker and darker than I remembered it. I blundered out onto a path which took me around the perimeter of a field planted with some unrecognisable crop. Then I came out at the old RAF base, once the centre of operations for the ammunition dump and now housing a silent and desolate industrial estate. I noted uneasily that one of the units had been taken over as the premises of a fireworks company, which was storing its stock in one of the old gypsum tunnels.

I turned back and retraced my steps. I began to wonder whether my memory was playing me false. Perhaps the enormous crater I saw in my memory would turn out to be a whole lot less impressive to my adult eye, just as the windswept expanses of a school playground or the woodlands of childhood have shrunk over the years. But in places there were signs of what lay beneath my feet: cryptic structures which I guessed must be disused ventilation shafts or access points into the tunnels. A herd of curious heifers crowded and jostled to watch as I kneeled on the grass and tried in vain to shove the iron cover aside for a glimpse down into one of them.

Again I entered dense woodland. It was tangled and shadowy and ominously quiet, like the setting for some macabre folktale. I tried to hack my way through and uphill, twisting my ankle on a root and ripping a hole in my jacket. The tearing sound made me jump. But I seemed to be making progress, it was lighter up ahead. Then suddenly I was standing at the foot of a metal fence secured to concrete posts, and topped with barbed wire, and signs warning of unexploded bombs. A while ago, long after all our picnicking and blackberrying and rolling down the hill, the Ministry of Defence carried out an investigation and concluded that there was still live ammunition in some of the surviving tunnels, and a risk of further explosions if any of the material was disturbed.

I edged around, keeping close to the line of the fence, until at last I arrived at a break in the trees, a sunlit patch of grass, and a jagged slab of polished white granite: a memorial to the dead, erected forty-six years after the event. A metal plaque bolted to the rock lists the names of all seventy known casualties, including eighteen whose bodies were never found and for whom the crater is their grave. I read down the list, noticing some surnames which were familiar from my own childhood: Brassington, Redfern, Bowring, Woolley, Fell. Then others which were not: Scuto, Di Paolo, Lanzoni, Trovato.

From here, there's a clear view across the crater. During the years since I was last here, the trees and bushes have seeded themselves and grown to fill the breach, like moss or thistles filling a hole in a field so that you don't notice it until your foot goes through. But in spite of all the burgeoning growth, this is still a gaping wound in the fabric: less raw than it was, but a permanent wound. The topography was changed forever in that moment of catastrophe. People spoke of running out of their shattered houses and standing frozen, disorientated, all the familiar landmarks gone and the usual ways between one place and the next destroyed.

The coroner charged with investigating the seventy deaths was John Lorimer Auden, cousin of the poet Wystan Hugh. He was a dignified and studious man, somewhat Edwardian in manner, known for his work as an amateur naturalist, most notably his study of molluscs. As coroner for the district, he made a solid contribution to public life and was well respected for his dedication and his readiness to see the good in people. It was Auden who, in the golden peacetime seven years earlier, had recommended Leonard Goodall to the Royal Humane Society for a bravery award. Now he had the fraught and frustrating job of making sense of what had happened at Fauld. On this occasion, too, his first instinct was to give credit for courageous behaviour. He was hampered in his search for answers by the secrecy surrounding the Air Ministry's own inquiry, but he pushed as hard as he could. 'Local inhabitants in the devastated area have behaved most admirably,' he wrote, 'and quite naturally they are anxious to have some information, and expect me to furnish it.'

Decency and determination were not enough to break through the official silence, however, and without the opportunity to examine the cause Auden had no alternative but to return a verdict of accidental death. The most likely explanation was that one of the workers in the exploder bay had chipped off a detonator with a steel chisel. But the inconclusive verdict created a vacuum which was quickly filled by rumours and conspiracy theories. The easiest target for blame were the Italian prisoners of war who had been drafted in to work in the tunnels, nine of whom died in the explosion. In some quarters they were suspected of an act of deliberate sabotage. Auden was quick to speak out in their defence, apologising for the slur on their good names and rebuking those who apportioned blame without the evidence to support it: 'The Italians did not ask to be sent to the dump. They only did their duty there. Following the explosion their lives became somewhat unpleasant in the district owing to what I can only call pot-house gossip.'

How can we know the person from the massed anonymous dead? Where should we listen for the faint signal of the individual? They are everywhere. Life rushed through them, they fell into the ground and were forgotten. The earth we walk on and depend on for food and shelter is made of them; they are our element. Only a few are enclosed within a church or cemetery wall, and still fewer have a stone marked with their name. The rest cannot be said to matter less. They were just as loved in their time. They are equal in significance. They are equal in insignificance.

Sixteen of the victims were from Tutbury, and I have seen their graves in the churchyard, close to Leonard's. When I went to visit Doug, he recalled the disaster and its aftermath in detail. He told me that the rear pews of the church had to be removed to make room for the rows of coffins awaiting burial. But it was the tunnels themselves he remembered best of all. His eyes glittered as he talked about the time he trespassed there as a youth: sneaked in alone and spent the whole night exploring by torchlight, then strolled out in the morning just as the men were arriving to start their day's work. He'd had plenty of adventures underground, but he'd never forget those tunnels. There were miles and miles of them, he said nostalgically.

Not long after the explosion, the war ended at last. A little later, in the traumatised landscape of the Stonepit Hills, gypsum extraction resumed, and continues to this day. The crater became a fact of life, a geographical feature, marked on Ordnance Survey maps and clearly visible on Google Earth. For relatives of the people who died here, it is a place of pilgrimage, and there's a service of commemoration each year attended by an Italian deputation as well as local villagers. When the dump went up, they all went with it – sergeant and private, farmer's daughter, prisoner of war. Death made no discrimination.

Within living memory, this was fields, farms and lanes, with a hidden underlife. A hole was blown in all that, and everything turned inside out. Even before they installed the memorial stone, this place had an indefinable atmosphere of loss. All I knew as a child was that it was an uncanny and overwhelming place to be, but it occurs to me now, standing here at the edge, that it always felt like a cemetery. From this spot I can see all the way across to the opposite side, to the point on the brink where I would have arrived after pedalling out from home on a summer afternoon like this one. I would drop my bike at the top, leave it on its side with the back wheel still spinning, and race down the steep slope into the mute strangeness of that other world. I can still see the trace of a path at the bottom, 400 feet below. When you got down there, everything was different. Sound was dulled, the air was tense and still. I would turn to look back along the route I'd taken, up and up the path, all the way to the lip of the crater, and feel a little stab of fear, as if I might be trapped here and never make it back.

Green

'It might make one in love with death, to think that one should be buried in so sweet a place.'

Percy Bysshe Shelley, *Adonaïs: An Elegy on the Death of John Keats*

Last year it occurred to me that I had reached a tipping point: I was going to more funerals than weddings. It's an ominous state of affairs. But the longer I thought about it, calling to mind recent examples of both, the more they seemed to have in common. The gathering of relatives who never meet at any other time, making for an altered sense of self, family and community. Music, flowers, the garrulous cousin who plies you with brandy. Shoe polish, tissues, good coat, secrets.

But something has changed. These occasions are not as predictable as they used to be. Not so long ago there were two kinds of wedding, church or registry office, and two kinds of funeral, church or crematorium. But recently I've been to weddings in a barn, a museum, a steam train and a donkey sanctuary. I have sat on a very scratchy bale of straw in the pouring rain while the couple made their vows under an umbrella which the wind kept turning inside out. And when my friend Sandra died two years ago, we followed in silence in our brightly coloured clothes behind her husband and sons as they carried the willow casket to a space between the trees, and lowered it into the ground themselves. I read a poem, someone else sang a song. I haven't been back to the place – mourning is not, in my case, attached to a specific location – but even if I did I wouldn't be able to find the exact spot because there are no head-stones or memorials there.

At its simplest, the 'natural' burial ground is a demarcated area near the edge of a cemetery, beyond the regular grass-mowing regime, a place with trees and wild flowers rather than head-stones. Less predictably, it may be a set-aside field on an arable farm, where the agricultural economy has diversified to make room for the planting of the dead; or a few acres of established woodland, bought or leased for the purpose. Some are run as prof-itable businesses, others as a labour of love. Those within a certain radius of London are becoming increasingly popular with city-dwellers looking to end up somewhere greener and more peaceful. Perhaps that desire was always there, but for all the usual reasons could not be fulfilled in life; now after death it becomes possible at last. Even the most ardent of urban souls might prefer to get out once the rat-race is run. After all, the alternatives are not ne-cessarily appealing. The lovely old churchyard is rarely an option, and would in any case come with a freight of religious associa-tions. The municipal cemetery can look vast and anonymous. If the special connection with birthplace and ancestral roots was severed a generation or two back, what's to stop people looking further afield?

The rise of natural burial since the 1970s has coincided with the growing awareness of environmental crisis. Sandra was born in London and lived there all her life. It was an urban existence, though she sought to balance it with walks in Richmond Park, holi-days in Cornwall, potted herbs on the windowsill. She was conscious of our human impact on the world, tried to avoid plas-tics and household chemicals, got about by bus and bicycle. I was not surprised by her choice of burial place, the instructions she jot-ted down in those last weeks, when she knew she was dying. The disappearing countryside, the destruction of wildlife, pollution and climate change, are problems so shocking in scale and potential consequence that it can be difficult to know how to live; perhaps the least we can do is arrange things so that we don't continue to do damage after death.

Cremation was once seen as the answer to all our problems in relation to the disposal of the dead. It was deeply unpopular to begin with, except among non-conformists like my own ancestors, and it took decades of persuasion before it really caught on. Now there are signs that the public mood is beginning to shift against it once more, this time because of the environmental price to be paid for all that burning, all those emissions. According to the natural death movement, the most ecologically sound method is a return to medieval practice: whole-body burial, wrapped simply in a shroud. Rather than taking measures to slow decomposition, we should let nature take its course: no embalming chemicals; and coffins or caskets, if they are used, made of sustainable and biodegradable materials such as cardboard or willow. We should be prepared to let go, to dissolve back into the earth, rather than clinging on to our mortal substance when life has gone from it.

Sandra's choice was partly motivated by her own environmental concerns. She had no religious faith, and there was no conflict with rituals or traditions. For her, this was about matching her deathstyle as closely as possible to her lifestyle. But the new natural burial grounds are more than just grave sites; they offer a way of doing the whole thing differently. They present a challenge to all the practices, professions and conventions around death. On their websites, there is a proliferation of alternatives available to the bereaved. You can help dig the grave, or back-fill it afterwards. You can push the coffin to the graveside on a hand-bier, or drive it there by horse and cart. You can weave personal mementoes into the willow casket, or stitch the shroud out of fleece sourced from a local flock. You can dispense entirely with the services of clergy and undertaker, say whatever words you like, plant a native tree, and stay on afterwards to picnic with friends and relatives. There are bucolic images on these websites, and picnics are mentioned again and again.

Behind the natural burial phenomenon lies a more general dissatisfaction with the whole funeral business: the top-hatted formality, the conveyor-belt blandness, the expense. Above all, the relinquishing of control into the cool hands of the professionals. My own experiences made me grateful for those cool hands, and content to delegate the smooth running of a debilitating public occasion. But there is talk of a 're-enchantment' of death, and for some people that means first recouping control, reasserting possession of the body. It means assuming the freedom to create a leave-taking which is individual, meaningful and in keeping with the memory of the deceased. Could there be anything further from the typical crematorium experience – the euphemistic architecture, the piped music, the theatricality of the curtains closing on the coffin – than carrying your loved one to their grave yourself, then sitting down on the grass with a picnic?

As that open-air wedding reminds me, the vagaries of British weather can make for a gulf between the vision and the reality. No one wants to picnic in the wind and rain. Similarly, there is a dissonance between the rural ideal and the actuality. Much of the English countryside – criss-crossed by motorways, stripped of its hedgerows, dotted with prefabricated buildings – does not resemble the dream in the heart of the lifelong city-dweller. 'Woodland burial' conjures a nostalgic image of grand old oak trees and dappled glades, but a wood takes time to grow, and if you're starting from scratch the first few years can look bleak: a bare field with rows of earth mounds, and thin saplings staked and stapled with protective mesh.

There are more than 200 natural burial grounds in Britain, each with its own ethos and its own aesthetic. Some look more or less traditional, each grave marked with a plaque or a small stone. Some have yielded to pressure and allow photographs, figurines, wind-chimes, plastic flowers. Others aim to blend in with the surrounding landscape, and forbid visible memorials of any kind. No stone, no wooden cross, no charms or tributes. The law requires exact records to be kept, but this can be done with minimal impact by embedding an electronic tag in the ground, or sinking a steel pole and using a metal detector to scan for the location of the grave.

My graveyard explorations are more about the unseen than the seen: the secret burials at the Harkirk, and of Agnes Gibbs at Blean; the inscrutable ground I paced over and over at St Ebbe's. The unmarked grave looks to me like a return to earlier practice, when a stone memorial was something only the rich could afford; the rest, like my own great-grandmother at Manor Park, were buried in common graves with nothing to show the place. The difference is that here in the natural burial ground it's a matter of choice. For some people, the very attraction is that it will allow them to disappear into the earth after their death, and to leave no visible sign. This speaks of a radical break with the past, a change in the way we see ourselves and our individual significance in space and time.

Where does it leave people like me, with my lifelong graveyard habit, my love of inscriptions, my fascination with the forgotten dead? These burial grounds cannot serve as repositories of individual stories, places of random discovery. You wouldn't come to them to study the past; here the past is consigned to the earth, and the earth is allowed to forget. Funerary practices are already changing in other ways too; the burial of cremated ashes, marked with rows of black marble plaques set into the grass, is falling out of favour. More than half are scattered instead, in some significant location like a park, hilltop or football pitch. (At least, that's the intention. The truth is that they are often kept in a state of limbo, under a bed or at the back of a wardrobe.) We are relinquishing the desire to etch every individual name on a stone. Perhaps there's a growing sense that we leave more than enough behind us already.

Whatever Shelley says, nothing can make death beautiful. Grief is a painful and messy business, and however gorgeous the view from the grave site the deceased is not there to see it. Still, there is a kind of comfort to be had by looking beyond the self, beyond our own horizons, and doing it right. 'Save the land for the living!' went the post-war slogan. But surely there are ways of rethinking our practices so that there's room on the same land for the living and the dead. We might in time return to the old practice of mowing our burial places for hay, managing them for timber, even sowing them with wheat. I'm on a train when I think of this, watching the imperfect fields and woods slip by. And suddenly I – who have never much cared what would become of my body after death – find to my surprise that I do care after all. I begin to consider breaking away from the practice of fire and wind so long established in my own family. I start to imagine another way. A piece of ground, somewhere, anywhere: the actual location is not important, and I would stake no claim to it. A simple rectangle of earth, tamped flush with the surface. The squares of turf neatly replaced, so that after a few weeks there's nothing to show it was ever disturbed at all.

Anguis fragilis

Someone has lost a copper bracelet in the long grass between forgotten graves. It may be very old, I think to myself, it may be treasure. I keep my eye fixed on its metallic gleam as I step carefully over the green glass chippings and traps of bramble.

But then it uncurls and is no longer a bracelet. It slides away elegantly under the green rafters, smooth as a trail of spilt liquid. It tracks through sunlight and shadow, pausing to flick out its notched tongue as if testing the air for the scent of prey.

It's a slow-worm, which is neither slow nor a worm, but a legless lizard, lover of the wild heath and the derelict plot. I knew them in childhood, and I remember the first time I saw one. We were walking on Cannock Chase, and I had run on ahead, kicking up dry leaves, when I saw that glancing movement at my feet and stopped dead. Felt, like Emily Dickinson, 'zero at the bone'. Then my dad caught up, saying no, it's not a snake, only a slow-worm.

Another day, there was one on a country lane in Devon, taking the afternoon sun. But when I looked more closely I saw a row of three puncture marks on its back, and knew it was dead, ambushed by a cat, who did not want to eat it but only to stop it with its claws.

They come in shades of silver and copper and steel and brass, polished to a glassy lustre, and some are dotted with sapphire or striped with jet, and if you uncover a nest of them the startled young ones zip around like streaks of light. Some people know them as blind-worms, but they are not blind. Neither do they sting, though Shakespeare had the three witches in *Macbeth* stir 'adder's fork, and blind-worm's sting' into the cauldron.

They are so often defined by what they are not. But they can, if they need to, redefine themselves: casting off the tail and making their escape, leaving it thrashing in the dust as a decoy for the crow or the magpie.

They will live in the compost heap, or under a sheet of corrugated tin or a piece of old carpet, though they are no longer a common sight in our orderly gardens and verges, or the brownfields cleared for housing estates.

But a churchyard is a refuge, one of the most biodiverse places we have left. Some are carefully managed for the purpose, with planned mowing and wildflower sowing, log piles and bat boxes. Even a well-kept graveyard can have some wilderness. In others, they benefit from human neglect. For slow-worms to thrive, we need do nothing. They are happy sheltering in the gaps in the wall and between fallen tombstones. They feed on slugs and worms, but before they can hunt they have to charge up in the sun, basking on a gravestone or burrowing into decaying vegetation for warmth. If they are not caught by a fox or a hedgehog, they can live for twenty years, sharing the churchyard with other refugees – firecrest, stag beetle, great crested newt, meadow-cranesbill. They breed and hunt in summer, hibernate in winter, as the old stones lean a little closer every year, and the mourners and dog-walkers come and go, and the ivy spreads its net in the yew.

Anguis fragilis, fragile snake, you survivor, you fluent thing which can take the shape of a horseshoe, a figure-of-eight, an iridescent scribble: our ancestors are buried under these stones, but yours are fossil.

I watch the metal glint of you disappear into the dark gap between slabs of granite, where I cannot follow.

Notes and Acknowledgements

I would like to thank all those who have provided help, advice and encouragement during the writing of this book, including Pat Barrow, John Beck, Mark Blundell, Caroline Hawkridge, Nicholas Hedges, Robert Minchin, Douglas Nash, Nigel Pantling, Michael Symmons Roberts, Ken and Larraine Worpole.

Old Haunts

There are numerous versions of the song 'Whenever you see a hearse go by', dating from at least the early 19th century. It has been passed down and altered through oral transmission and therefore qualifies, no less than 'The Banks of the Sweet Primroses', as a folk song.

In *The Work of the Dead*, Thomas Laqueur examines the ways in which the dead and the living interact and depend on one another, and the particular role played by burial sites: 'Bodies create a community of memory; visitors to these bodies confirm it; together they make a claim on space and on the attention of the living.'

By Flaming Tortures Tried

In the course of my background reading, I was surprised to find the Pickett tomb and its inscriptions mentioned in *The History and Antiquities of the Parish of Stoke Newington* by William Robinson. This well-respected work, published forty years after the event, gives a description so specific and detailed I might have believed Robinson had transcribed it himself direct from the stone, except that it's quite different from what's actually there.

The Harkirk

I am grateful to the British Museum for arranging access to the Harkirk burial register and William Blundell's notebook.

The notebook habit was continued by subsequent generations of Blundells. I enjoyed *Crosby Records: A Cavalier's Note Book*, edited by T. E. Gibson, in which William Blundell's grandson (also William) gives intriguing glimpses of his everyday life as well as his military exploits in the Civil War. There is an instruction for dyeing hair 'by rubbing with the light dust of cork which is burnt to ashes'; a bill for his daughter's new clothes, including £2.17.00 for 'a sky-coloured silk mohair coat'; and a method for luring crows by tethering one along with a kite and allowing them to attack each other ('Remember that you tie up one foot of your kite to make the battle more equal').

The site William chose for his burial ground may have carried extra significance at the time. According to D. R. Woolf in 'Little Crosby and the horizons of early modern historical culture' (*The Historical Imagination in Early Modern Britain*, edited by D. R. Kelley and D. H. Sacks): 'In modern historical thinking, time must precede space, the moment of occurrence go before its location … but not for the antiquaries of the late sixteenth century, who began with locations, rather than events'. The recusant community had to make do with unconsecrated ground for their graveyard, but 'the phantom Saxon church helped to soften the ad hoc character of the arrangement'.

Forever

Frederick Burgess's classic study, *English Churchyard Memorials*, has been an invaluable source of knowledge throughout the writing of this book.

Rapparee

My thanks to Ilfracombe Museum for information and advice.

In his book *Slaves of Rapparee*, Pat Barrow tells the story of his 'obsession' with the wreck of the *London* in his own words.

Robert Hawker's stories about 'Cruel Coppinger' were first published in Charles Dickens's magazine *Household Words* in 1866. The sea mist drifts not only over the Reverend Hawker's writings, but also over the man himself. He was certainly an eccentric, but some of the more colourful details may have been invented by Sabine Baring-Gould, author of *The Vicar of Morwenstow*, a 'biography' he later admitted was semi-fictional. We cannot know whether it's true, as Hawker claims, that Coppinger ordered his wife to hide a bundle of contraband silk in the oven, then beat her when it burnt to ashes. Neither is it clear whether or not Hawker tricked the locals by disguising himself as a mermaid, sitting on the rocks singing and combing his hair; or whether he excommunicated a cat, or hanged a mouse for breaking the Sabbath. Myth grows on myth. Tangible and still standing, however, is the driftwood hut he built on the cliff above Sharpnose Point, where he would go to write poetry, smoke opium and watch the sea.

In *The Wreck at Sharpnose Point*, Jeremy Seal tells of a visit to Galsham, the farmhouse on the cliffs at Welcombe, where he sees for himself the piece of broken window-glass scratched with the signature of 'D.H. Copinger'.

Oh Lovely Child

A version of 'Oh Lovely Child' was published in 1845, under the heading 'Early Death a Blessing', in *A Cypress Wreath for the Grave of a Young Person* by the Rev. John Bruce, Minister of Liverpool Necropolis. The purpose of this volume – part anthology, part religious tract – was to comfort and strengthen grieving parents, at a time when their experience was near-universal. In his Introduction, Bruce writes that 'few parents have been spared the anguish of watching by the side of the death-bed of one or more of their children ... the fresh green sod is most frequently broken into, and the sepulchre is newly made, to receive, as its first inhabitant, the youngest of the family'.

The cases of Amelia and Richard are mentioned by Elizabeth Hurren in 'The business of anatomy and being poor: Why have we failed to learn the medical and poverty lessons of the past?', from *Being Poor in Modern Europe*, eds. Inga Brandes, Andreas Gestrich. I learned a great deal about the historical context by reading Ruth Richardson's *Death, Dissection and the Destitute*.

Carole Newbigging, who has lived on the Blackbird Leys estate all her life, has written about it from the inside, giving a very different view which challenges the stereotyping and vilification. Her book *The Changing Faces of Blackbird Leys* documents the growth of a new community: its playgrounds and community centres, street parties, sports days and school productions. Her story fizzes with the energy of determined individuals who brought people together and made things happen, on limited or non-existent resources.

My thanks to the Oxfordshire History Centre at Cowley Library.

The Rosary

Nick Williams is a fount of knowledge about the Rosary, and I am grateful for his book *The Rosary Cemetery, Norwich: A Place of Decent Interment. Norwich in the Nineteenth Century*, edited by Christopher Barringer, helped me understand what the city was like in John Barker's time; and R. H. Mottram's *If Stones Could Speak* brings the place to life through the fabric of its streets, inns and churchyards.

One of many stories related by John Barker's friend and contemporary Lord George Sanger, in his gloriously colourful autobiography *Seventy Years a Showman*, takes place in 1850 when he takes over a disused chapel near the Strand, which he plans to use as a theatre. However, he moves out hastily when he discovers that the bodies of 12,000 paupers are stacked in a vault under the floor. The chapel later becomes a dancing saloon, and the enterprising owner does his best to turn its ghastly history into an attraction, with handbills advertising 'Dancing on the Dead – Admission Threepence. No lady or gentleman admitted unless wearing shoes and stockings'.

Thomas Murphy's *History of the Showmen's Guild* indicates the surprising mixture of characters who made a living in the fairground business, and the range of trades which depended on it. In 1892, the Van Dwellers' Association extended honorary membership to 'Lessees of Show Grounds, Circus and Theatre Proprietors, Wagon Builders, Wood Carvers, Painters, Artistes, Gilders, Tilt Makers, Horse Dealers, Harness Makers, Lamp Makers, Roundabout Constructors, Organ Builders, Musical Instrument Manufacturers, Electric and other Engineers, Animal and Bird Merchants, Gun Makers, Printers, Bill Posters, Confectionery, Toy and Fancy Merchants, Uniform Tailors, and others'.

The ride that made John Barker's name is pictured in *The Circular Steam Switchback* by Kevin Scrivens and Stephen Smith.

My thanks to Norfolk Record Office, and to the newspaper archive at Norfolk and Norwich Millennium Library.

Ruin

Rose Macaulay's masterpiece *Pleasure of Ruins* was often on my mind as I explored London's sprawling Victorian cemeteries. Graveyards are not her subject, but they do haunt the text at times. Writing about ancient sites in the Peloponnese, for instance, she describes the layers of archaeology as 'the ghosts of dead ages sleeping together'.

Saint Agnes of Blean

The story of Agnes Gibbs is mentioned fleetingly in *The Kent Village Book* by Alan Bignell.

Bright and Sad

Sir Oswald Mosley published his *History of the Castle, Priory &
Town of Tutbury* in 1832. He ascribes the writing of the book to
a 'fortuitous circumstance': the discovery the previous summer of
the hoard of ancient coins in the River Dove. This find 'naturally
produced in the public mind a degree of curiosity to know how
they became deposited there, and the enquiry was so intimately
connected with the ancient history of Tutbury, as to call forth a
universal demand for some publication respecting it'. The book,
ponderous and rollicking by turns, portrays a town famous not
only for its castle and priory but also for its drinking, brawling and
bull-running, and for the wedding of Robin Hood to a local girl
called Clorinda. This Sir Oswald was the great-great-grandfather
of the fascist of the same name who came to notoriety in the 1930s.
The housing estate where I was born was built on what had been
the lawns of the Mosley family home; we used to walk up the road
and peer through the fancy gates at what was left of the old Hall.

My special thanks to the Family and Local History Centre at
Burton Library where, as it happens, my father was Librarian for
many years.

Dust

The story of the Fauld disaster is told by those who witnessed it in
Voices from the Explosion by Valerie Hardy, who was a child at
the time and whose family farm was badly damaged in the blast.

Green

Natural Burial, by Andy Clayden, Trish Green, Jenny Hockey and
Mark Powell, is a serious, humane and inspirational study of this
different way of caring for the dead.

penguin.co.uk/vintage